THE COMPLETE HOME OFFICE

THE COMPLETE
HOME OFFICE

Planning Your Work Space
for Maximum Efficiency

Alvin Rosenbaum

VIKING
STUDIO
BOOKS

VIKING STUDIO BOOKS
Published by the Penguin Group
Penguin Books USA Inc., 375 Hudson Street,
New York, N. Y. 10014 U. S. A.
Penguin Books Ltd, 27 Wrights Lane,
London W8 5TZ, England
Penguin Books Australia Ltd, Ringwood,
Victoria, Australia
Penguin Books Canada Ltd, 10 Alcorn Avenue
Toronto, Ontario, Canada M4V 3B2
Penguin Books (N. Z.) Ltd, 182–190 Wairau Road,
Auckland 10, New Zealand

Penguin Books Ltd Registered Offices:
Harmondsworth, Middlesex, England

First published in 1995 by Viking Penguin,
a division of Penguin Books USA Inc.

10 9 8 7 6 5 4 3 2 1

Illustration credits appear on pages 217–218.

Rosenbaum, Alvin.
        The complete home office : planning your work space for maximum
        efficiency / Alvin Rosenbaum.
                    p.   cm.
        Includes index.
        ISBN 0–670–85293–7
        1. Office layout. 2. Office decoration. 3. Office furniture. 4. Offices—Location. 5. Home-based
        businesses. I. Title.
HF5547.2.R67   1995
658.2'3—dc20   94–45190

Printed in Singapore
Set in Adobe Garamond

Designed by Alvin Rosenbaum and Jennifer Cosgrove

CONTENTS

NORTH ELEVATION

PREFACE

Coming home after a hot, three-day road trip, I pick up my mail and Federal Express packages by the front door and descend to my office, which is located behind and below our family's living area in a space we built off the main structure over five years ago. Entering the office, I see that several faxes have arrived and are curled in a roll, and I remember that I vowed to investigate the purchase of a plain paper fax machine weeks ago.

Sitting down, I immediately log on to First Class, the electronic mail system used by my firm. While I sometimes read and send electronic mail on the road, my motel room outside Altoona did not have a convenient way to plug into a telephone line. Often, while traveling with my laptop computer, I will log-on to download files and messages, send faxes, and work on memos that I started at the office. I do this all on the fly, at airport lounges, in someone else's office, or early in the morning from my lodgings.

Built-ins provide the greatest utilization of space, which is often at a premium in apartments. Interior designer Patricia Eichman renovated the Old Citrus Soap Factory in downtown San Diego, *opposite*, for model apartments in the City Front Terrace condominium complex.

Entry to the author's Chevy Chase, Maryland, home office, *above*.

I retrieve a package a messenger left in the back door and note that a manuscript was left by a freelancer who came by while I was gone. I check my telephone's voice mail, but discover only one message since I had checked it only a few minutes before from my cellular phone. While it is often difficult to find an available line for data communications on the road, voice lines are abundant and I check my telephone messages throughout the day, returning calls as I find the time, usually to other people's voice mail. I rarely use my cellular phone for returning calls, but reserve it for retrieving messages while I'm in my car or calling enroute when I'm on my way home or late for a meeting.

Having departed my home office in a rush, I find that the accumulated mail and faxes, together with the clutter of research materials that I left out, have quickly gotten out of control in the few minutes since I returned. Three copies each of the *Washington Post*, *Wall Street Journal*, and *New York Times* are stacked on the floor, awaiting my review. A colleague who works for me part time has come and gone that morning, leaving me a note regarding a production issue that requires immediate attention. Out my window, I see a carpenter twenty feet away, preparing to cut a 2 x 4 with a radial saw to repair a broken rail. The noise will be annoying, but I'm glad to see that the work is finally going forward.

Just as I begin to sort out the mess, my younger son, five-year-old Sam, returns from swimming lessons and pops down to my office, greeting me with a hug, receiving an action figure that I purchased at a Pennsylvania toy store, then disappearing for his afternoon play date. Through chaos and quiet, I plow through my accumulated desk work in an hour, turning then to prepare an expense report and to write a thank-you note for hospitality received on my journey.

My home office provides two vistas, out my window onto Rock Creek Park and, through a myriad of devices, out to the world. My home office also provides refuge, a quiet place for work and contemplation, a place to read, write, and communicate, whether it be a face-to-face meeting, a call from my older son's office, or a fax from my client in Tokyo.

Creating the perfect office space that would enable me to be as productive, creative, and comfortable as possible was the goal that I set prior to developing a home office in 1991. Although I had been self-employed in my own business for nearly two decades, I had only worked from home since 1989, which was barely enough time to gain enough experience to avoid serious mistakes.

Working as a writer and strategic planning consultant for many years, my ability to work either alone or with a small staff has moved in tandem with the evolution of computer and telecommunications technology. My home office today is a direct result of advances made in the 1980s that permitted me to downsize my downtown Washington, D.C., office from an average of twelve employees to an office of four professionals by 1989 to no employees at all, then back up to a small professional staff. I have moved from an office of 3,500 square feet to 1,200 square feet to a home office of about 450 square feet. My office is now networked with that of my older son and business partner Aaron, whose office is two miles away. He and his colleagues are connected to my home office by an ISDN line that supports a network of databases, e-mail, and the Internet so that we can be in constant and instantaneous communication with one another.

For each business or profession, the impact of computerization and other technological advances on productivity has varied widely. But for virtually every kind of knowledge worker—from mortgage banker to architect, insurance broker to bond trader—the effects of digital devices have been wide and deep. They have made impressive inroads into worker satisfaction and productivity and have provided an extraordinary degree of workplace flexibility, leading to decreased stress, closer family life, and, for many, a much happier existence than was possible as a commuting office worker.

As a small businessman for most of my career, the move home was a natural extension of other business decisions to focus my work on fewer projects without the unrelenting pressure of producing a payroll every other week. Having met more than 400 payrolls over eighteen years, I had a serious case of burnout and sought only to find pleasant clients with interesting problems that I could either solve myself or solve with a little help from a few, but not more than several, friendly collaborators.

At first I was not at all sure that the transition to home was a permanent move since it was difficult to project the impact on my income. Moving from the management of others to the management of my own time, I felt relatively sure that I would come to work early and stay late if necessary. I thoroughly enjoyed all aspects of my work and simply wanted more time to do it, spending less time as an administrator/manager and more time providing services to clients.

As I began to plan my new home office from my temporary basement setup, I realized that I would have to enlarge the space of our house rather than simply redecorate an existing space. Knowing that it would be a long, expensive project, I was determined to get the most from my efforts. By planning the new space at ground level, the roof of my home office could become a deck off the living area of the floor above.

Although I am not an architect, I had studied architecture during college and have written on design subjects over the years. As I planned my new home office I discovered that while there were dozens of titles on starting home-based businesses and other work-from-home issues, there were literally no books on the subject of home office design.

I have written *The Complete Home Office* to fill that gap. To help me along the way, I am grateful to my agent, Alan Kellock, who found a sympathetic publisher, Michael Fragnito, who helped me shape the book. I am also grateful to my editor at Viking Studio Books, Martha Schueneman; to Harriet Baker, who helped me research the subject from her home office in San Diego; to Dan Elasky, who provided editorial assistance; to Marcy Mermel, Eli Castro, and Janet Rumbarger who helped me put the book to bed. I also wish to thank Mark Schurman and Steve Chappell from Herman Miller Inc., who went beyond the call of duty to help me understand the home office marketplace.

Traditional libraries and home studies can easily be converted into home offices with adaptable furniture. This arrangement cleverly hides computer equipment, wiring, and other evidence of business-related activity.

Finally, I wish to thank my son, Aaron, now also my business partner, who has guided me from the beginning, and even before the beginning, through the technological morass, to a place and time that I could not even imagine a few years ago. My newly found freedom and productivity are offshoots of this new digital age. Without Aaron's continuing help and encouragement, my home office and my new working life would not have been possible. As a pathfinder and visionary, Aaron Rosenbaum is now creating systems and ways of work that will help society find new, more productive and pleasant ways to perform its work in new and varied workplaces. His work in telecommunications, including wireless and remote-access strategies, is helping to shape an extraordinary array of new choices for our lives. To Aaron, with love and with gratitude, I dedicate this book.

INTRODUCTION

Working at home can significantly contribute to your efficiency while providing wonderful opportunities to improve the quality of your home and family life. Nearly 39 million people in the United States and Canada earn at least part of their income from a home office base, a number that is increasing by nearly four million per year.

Home office workers fall into four main categories: They are either self-employed, operating a part-time or full-time business from home; are working part time for an outside company; are telecommuters, working at home full time for an outside company; or are working at a full-time job outside their home but maintaining a home office for early morning, evening, and weekend work related to their job.

Home Office Demographics

According to Link Resources Corporation, a New York-based market research firm, about twelve million people work out of their home full time, with an additional 10.5 million who moonlight. Five and a half million workers have become telecommuters, with another 10.6 million who work in conventional offices but also work at home after hours or on weekends. Taken together, more than one in three American adults work at home at least part of the time.

Home-based businesses are also tracked by the Census Bureau, which reports:
- 11.8 million Americans operate businesses from their homes.
- 25 percent of all incorporated businesses in the United States are home-based.
- Of the two million U.S. businesses having employees, 20 percent are home-based.
- 20 percent of all businesses with gross sales of more than $100,000 per year are based in family dwellings or apartments.

According to the Bureau of Labor Statistics, the typical home office worker is white and married: 20 percent of white workers perform more than half of their work at home, compared with only 9 percent of blacks and 8 percent of Hispanics. Only 21 percent of all home office workers live alone, compared with 27 percent of all workers. While more men than women work at home, women are twice as likely to work at home full time. Mary Brouder, a demographer for The Roper Organization, suggests that this trend will continue because "women are interested in the advantage of being able to combine work and family."

An increasing number of home offices are professionally designed or incorporate furniture developed for the home office environment. For the self-employed and for others who work full time at home and who receive clients in their home office, greater attention must be paid to the comfort, functionality, and ambience of the space.

Builder magazine, published by the National Association of Home Builders, reports that more than half of home workers have college degrees (one in five holding postgraduate degrees), and that home office workers have household incomes more than $10,000 higher than the national average.

Home office workers spent more than $30 billion on home office electronics and telephone services in 1993. With the cost of technology decreasing rapidly, companies like AT&T, Sharp, and Canon can offer progressively faster and better equipment and service for less cost. Indeed, this downward spiral is having a great impact on the number of people working at home.

Increasingly, the modern home office revolves around a workstation with a computer and telephone and is organized according to several variables: the type of work performed, the presence of children in the household, the hours in use, the number of people who occupy the office, and its setting and neighborhood. The size, location, and style of home offices are determined largely by the stage of development of a worker's career and by his or her attitude about working at home. With children running in and out, noises from the yard, and whiffs of chicken soup emanating from the kitchen, most households are ill-equipped and poorly organized to accommodate a fully functional and professional office.

Recognizing the increasing use of home offices, the Internal Revenue Service has recently developed an optional form, "Expenses for Business Use of Your Home," which is used by approximately four million taxpayers, in addition to those who will continue to use the Schedule C form to declare home office deductions.

A number of socioeconomic factors has led to a tremendous increase in the number of home office workers: the trend toward corporate downsizing and the creation of "virtual" organizations, the high cost of real estate and the brutality of global competitiveness, the decentralization of work, the reemphasis on the family in American culture, and environmentalism.

As the work-at-home community grows, a significant number have been identified as affluent, both as full-time consultants and entrepreneurs, and as executives who simply spend part of their week working from home.

These up-market, over-40-year-old workers are part of a downsizing trend in corporate upper-middle management, including early retirees with pensions or severance cash. These legions of high-tech, high-energy executives are making significant changes in the home office culture. They are investing in quality products

Carolin Schebish designed an area at home that is shared with her husband and is adjacent to living spaces. This office is presentable to clients as well as functional, with work and living spaces demarcated by an area rug and dropped ceiling.

Differing work habits require different solutions: some workers need a room of their own, while others can share; some workers need peace and quiet, while others wish to be in the middle of household activities; some workers prefer a homelike setting for their office, while others prefer the look of a traditional office environment.

and high-end services, creating whole new categories for manufacturers. As with telecommuters, the older, more affluent home office worker is emerging as a leading consumer of high-end home office furniture and equipment. As a parallel workplace trend, sales executives who have maintained regional or branch offices for an occasional meeting but, more often, as a place for making telephone calls are moving in droves into home offices as corporations begin to economize, closing sales offices across the country.

For the telecommuter—the home worker who has an employer but communicates with the office electronically—the freedom to bring work home can become the burden of working more hours with seemingly less recognition for the same compensation. Corporations that are exploring telecommuting as a cost-saving, employee-pleasing benefit often seek direct and indirect ways to regulate employee activity at home to monitor productivity and promote connections between home and office. Telework consultants emphasize the separation of home life and work life as if it were church and state: employees should dress for work, keep regular hours, maintain complete separation between home and home office, and generally behave as if they were still working at the office. Office furniture and equipment are being redesigned to fit a new scale for the home, bringing the science of organization and pristine efficiency, ergonomics, acoustics, illumination, and a dazzling array of telecommunications and data processing devices and services to our basements and spare bedrooms.

New York apartments are perhaps the toughest home office design projects because they usually contain only small spaces that serve multiple functions. Interior designer Joan Halperin reconfigured a two-bedroom Manhattan apartment, *opposite* and *above*, to work more comfortably as a residence and home office for a couple with two children. The built-in shelving doubles as a long credenza that hides a television set, *above*.

By day this home office is really the entire apartment, while it also functions as a comfortable home during off-hours.

The thirty-minute journey from home to office by a single commuter in his or her fossil-fueled vehicle—the standard American trip to work for nearly half a century—may become more of a rarity as the Clean Air Act begins to mandate mass transit and car pooling, as roads continue to become even more clogged, and as the rate of construction of new office space in major center cities continues to decline. Spawned in part by technology, much of American society has been moving away from its urban office moorings for more than four decades.

In the past home offices have tended to be afterthoughts, small and cluttered, inefficient and uninviting. Dozens of books and articles have provided tips on *setting up* a home office, as if it were a task for a Saturday afternoon rather than a project that may have enormous consequences on your life, relating not only to your income but to your sanity at work and the time you have left to spend with your family.

THE COMPLETE HOME OFFICE

Frank Lloyd Wright believed in the integration of work and family life, and designed his Usonian houses (beginning in the mid-1930s) to include studies, sanctums, and workshops. In this 1975 photograph, Professor Stanley Rosenbaum (the author's father) works at his desk correcting papers in his house that Wright designed for the Rosenbaums in 1940.

Wright achieved spatial integration of living and working areas by changing ceiling and floor levels at the transition from one area to the next, but leaving entryways open and using bookshelves or other cabinetry as a bridge between spaces.

A Brief History of the Home Office

Thomas Jefferson worked from his house and would feel right in place in today's American home office. At Monticello, Jefferson produced an enormous number of books and essays, entreaties and voluminous correspondence. He invented a lap desk—the colonial counterpart of a laptop computer—that permitted him to read and write as he traveled the long road between Charlottesville and Washington and the eastern ports.

In Jefferson's day, most of the houses of the gentry contained libraries, some with vast book-lined rooms with gilded ceilings and pocket doors that perhaps included an elaborate Chinese secretaire by Thomas Chippendale or an ingenious writing desk by Thomas Sheraton. Those who worked in the trades often combined their home and office: a family lived over its storefront butcher shop or haberdashery.

At the turn of the nineteenth century the middle class began to grow, and the formality of the great houses gave way to a more relaxed family style. Society's burled veneer libraries—once male-dominated retreats—became more like contemporary family rooms. But the need for a hideaway persisted, and by the 1840s American houses began to include a smaller room known as the study. Even at the White House, what had once been the president's office—the second floor Oval Room—became the family's informal living room.

For wives and mothers, the hideaway was often a sewing room if they were middle class, or a small sitting room off a boudoir for ladies of leisure. By this century, both study and sewing room were folded into a space that became known as the den, often containing a desk for bill paying and letter writing, a quiet refuge from the commotion of the dining room or the stifling formality of the parlor or living room. By the 1950s, television had totally transformed the den into an all-purpose family or recreation room where children played on the linoleum floor and informal TV dinners were served on trays. Any semblance of the peace and quiet of the old den or study was gone forever.

Only a few architects at mid-century paid homage to the concept of a home office as refuge. Frank Lloyd Wright consistently included spaces on his house plans for rooms that were tucked away—a sanctum or retreat, or simply a study or shop—even within his small Usonian houses.

Beginning with the introduction of Art Deco furniture in the 1920s, some office desks and chairs were designed to blend into residential decors. Modernism, including all of its styles from the 1920s through the 1960s, contributed to a blurring of home and office decors within a narrow range of highly styled, sophisticated furniture that found its way into a few American homes. For the most part, however, the contrast between work and home could not have been greater. As Modernism invaded corporate offices with efficient, streamlined architecture and furniture, the American home remained traditional, with homeowners favoring Colonial, Queen Anne, then Empire and Victorian detailing, furniture, and fabrics.

There have always been millions of home offices hidden away in America homes. Writers and artists, film and television producers, graphic and interior designers, architects, lawyers, farmers, and doctors have made their offices or ateliers at home in recent times. In addition, home crafts have flourished, including a preponderance

of wood shops, mechanics' garages, tinkers' benches, florists' greenhouses, and musicians' studios, all variations on the theme of the home office.

What once was the purview of only the very rich, the arty, or the famous—an entire room completely planned and designed to be an efficient workplace at home—is now simply becoming part of the American scene: dwellings in the country, the suburbs, and the city now have the same capability of communicating with the world that only the biggest companies in the richest countries did a few years ago.

Home office furniture from Herman Miller from the 1940s and 1960s, *opposite* **and** *right,* **was some of the very first modern furniture manufactured in America. It was scaled for the home but retained features appropriate to the new architecture of the era.**

The Situation Today

A few companies are now mandating home offices. In California, for example, Regulation 15 requires companies with more than 100 employees in some parts of the state to prepare plans to reduce the number of automobile trips. Federal legislation under the Clean Air Act has similar provisions for targeted areas in California, Connecticut, Delaware, Illinois, Indiana, Maryland, New Jersey, New York, Pennsylvania, Texas, and Wisconsin, where automobile emissions and industrial pollution pose serious air quality problems. Many companies are planning to encourage their employees to telecommute in order to comply with these new regulations.

While some would argue that it is primarily environmental issues compelling the move toward home offices, other analysts point to a more common rationale for the increase in corporate telecommuting strategies: reduced costs and improved profits, as well as a desire to hire and/or retain valuable employees.

Southern California architect Michael Lehrer was charged with remaking this casual, eclectic house on a Hollywood hilltop. His clients, a writer/producer/director and his wife, an actress/painter/sculptor, asked him to keep the spirit of the existing house while modifying and adding to it. Lehrer added light, views, and open space, especially in the ultradramatic writer's tower.

Downsizing is another reason. Many companies are converting permanent employees to contingent workers, in essence pushing them out the door but often protecting them with contracts or promises of freelance work. In some cases these arrangements become permanent; other workers may wander off to another job, retire, or start new businesses.

For the fully employed telecommuter, the home office is an extension of the main office and is even, in a few cases, planned by a facilities manager and furnished and equipped through the company's purchasing department.

Employer-initiated and employer-generated home offices are a large percentage of the total of new home offices and are a growing sector of the home office sphere. AT&T calculates that there are twenty million corporate home workers—about half of the total—with an annual growth rate of 7 percent. Self-employed home workers are also growing but at half that rate of growth. Among these home office workers an indeterminate number are part-time workers, or full-time workers occupying their home office only part of the time.

The ten million self-employed home office workers include technical and creative professionals who work on

contract, entrepreneurs, and small business owners. A small percentage in each category work at home because they are disabled.

These two basic worker groups—employees and the self-employed—are further distinguished by those who view their situation as temporary and/or forced and a much larger group for whom working at home is a blessing. Most reluctant home office workers eventually re-enter the workaday world at an office (or retire). The rest continue on in their home offices, motivated by their career success and increased enjoyment of recreational pursuits and family life.

Workers whose jobs centered on the production of information—writers, editors, graphic designers, and software producers—have always preferred the independence and solitude permitted by home-based offices or studios. A second category of traditional home-based professionals are physicians, particularly psychiatrists and psychologists, lawyers, accountants, and various kinds of consultants. A third category for home-based work are those whose work is nomadic—notably salespeople—who travel most of the time and have only limited requirements for an office. Finally, marketing, legal,

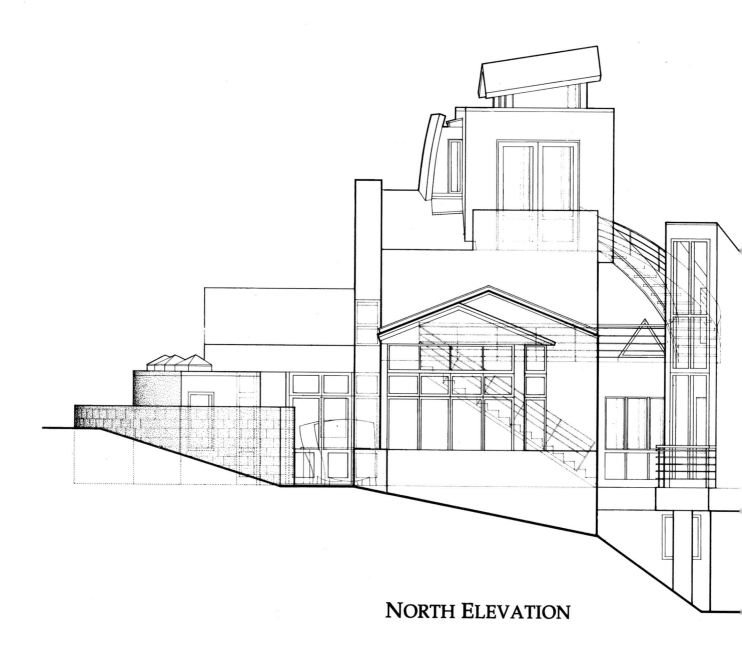

NORTH ELEVATION

While Virginia Woolf demanded only a room of her own, other writers demand more. The "skybox" that sits atop this Hollywood home provides spectacular panoramic views.

financial, and technological services are becoming increasingly place-independent, streamlined, and ultraefficient.

According to Secretary of Labor Robert B. Reich, America's workforce is now divided into *routine production services, in-person services,* and *symbolic-analytic services.* It is this third category that is both expanding in opportunity—as the information economy engulfs the world—and is also changing in a manner that permits, perhaps even encourages, home-based work strategies. Reich defines these workers as engaged in "problem-identifying, problem-solving, and strategic brokering activities," trading in "data, words, oral, and visual representations."

The professions encompassed by symbolic-analytic services include engineers, scientists, public relations executives, investment bankers, real estate developers, architects, interior and landscape designers, graphic artists, management consultants, strategic planners, system analysts and programmers, headhunters, musicians, professors, journalists, film producers, marketing consultants, and publishers. These workers rely more on technology and less on their immediate surroundings and face-to-face contacts to accomplish their work. They also may consider the prestige and location of their workplace less relevant to their ability to do their work or to attract and impress clients.

Home office furniture, *below,* is often designed to blend with traditional home furnishings or with detailing of no specific or distinctive style. Other home offices, particularly those of professionals with frequent visitors, may seek to replicate downtown office settings that are not intended to blend with the surrounding residential furnishings, *opposite.*

Four Fellow Travelers

As we explore the complexities and choices involved in planning, designing, equipping, and furnishing a home office, we will frequently look in on four professional people who maintain home offices. Each of these persons is a fictional composite based on my interviews and typifies one of the four major categories of home office user. By examining their decision-making processes and solutions as they confront their home office needs, we can better understand how to make the right choices in designing our own offices. Our four colleagues and their home office categories are:

- **Greg Simpson:** full-time employee with a part-time office at home
- **Melinda Davidson:** self-employed with a small-scale home office
- **Elizabeth Haskell:** self-employed with a large, separate home office
- **Jim Forrest:** telecommuter with a full-time home office

In order to provide contexts for our subsequent visits with these four professionals throughout the book, we need to look briefly at their employment circumstances and their reasons for establishing home offices.

Attics are often difficult and expensive to convert, but may offer extraordinary views and expansive space for a home office. Often the problem with attic home offices is access. A full-width stairway that meets building code and is suitable for daily office traffic and visitors may require too much floor space on the story below.

For **Greg Simpson**, a 29-year-old single sales executive for a Baltimore high-tech firm, having an office at home permits him to work out at a gym every morning and to coach a settlement house basketball league in the late afternoons and early evenings.

At his office near Harbor Square, Greg was constantly playing politics, striving for raises and a more senior position by sitting in on strategy sessions and networking with the firm's brass. After three years of limited success, he decided to build a reputation as a star producer rather than simply a team player. Committed "to the field," he now spends as little time as possible in his new home office, calling on prospects and paying regular visits to his existing clients to build their loyalty to him and increase his accounts.

There are risks to his strategy, and he is not sure how it will work out. His home office is in an alcove off his kitchen in a high-rise apartment, and he is not interested in investing in more elaborate furniture or equipment; his laptop computer, cellular phone, and office chair belong to the firm.

Greg loves the kind of flexibility that comes with a home office. The only problem that might drive him back to the office is his sense of isolation. Greg has always been part of a team, from Cub Scouts to fraternity basketball, and he feels alone. He is dating less and worries that he'll never get married.

Melinda Davidson has a different home office story. A graphic designer for twelve years at a Fortune 500 corporation headquartered in New York's Westchester County, she was let go in 1990, but with the promise of freelance work from her former boss. Melinda was given ten months' salary—nearly $40,000—as severance pay, and she budgeted $10,000 of that to build an office in a maid's room, a ten-by-twelve-foot space off the kitchen with its own bathroom and outside entrance. The room had been used for storage since she and her husband purchased the house in 1986.

Melinda's home office purchases (not included in the $10,000 construction budget) included some furniture and a Macintosh computer, scanner, printer, and software. She believed that as a freelancer she could recapture half her income from her former employer and then make up the remainder from new accounts. Unfortunately, with the recession, 1991 was a financial disaster for Melinda. Her total freelance income amounted to only $9,500, with all but $1,500 coming from her former employer. Her Macintosh was mostly given over to proposals and résumé-writing. Her usual self-confidence was shattered.

The next year was a different story. She refocused her marketing efforts from corporate work to publishing after a former colleague asked her to design an illustrated book. She liked the work and was able to get several more projects, finishing the year with a net income after expenses of $33,000. She also purchased a photocopier and a new workstation for her home office. Melinda enjoys working with her new clients and hopes to add another publisher to her two-client roster soon.

While Greg and Melinda established their home offices quickly, propelled by circumstances, **Elizabeth Haskell** of Nashville, a 48-year-old accountant, planned hers for nearly five years before making her move, just in time to watch the last of her three children head off to college. "As the most junior member of a six partner firm, I always went my separate way," Elizabeth explained. "While my partners were all into big, lucrative real estate deals in the 1980s, I plodded along working with small medical practices around the university."

Elizabeth and her family live on a shaded street near Vanderbilt University Hospital in an area where there are home offices on every block. Doctors, chiropractors, dentists, lawyers, musicians, and songwriters work from bungalows built before World War II. Many have big yards and beautiful gardens.

Elizabeth resigned from her firm in 1993 and moved into a spacious three-room suite that she'd had built behind her house. She enlarged the parking area adjacent to her office to accommodate four cars and landscaped the area so that the entrance to her office is clearly separate from her home. The office itself was designed and built by a friend of hers in the construction business; it includes a large office with a conference area, a smaller room with two workstations, a tiny waiting area, and a lavatory. When Elizabeth and her husband retire, they plan to market the house to a dentist or psychiatrist with a home-based practice. In planning, Elizabeth realized that her needs were similar to those of a small medical office, which was also the client network she served. She even roughed in plumbing for a sink (which was behind the lavatory off the waiting area) so that a doctor's examination room could be added later. The total cost of the office was $51,000.

Elizabeth believes that the economics of her practice will change only slightly, as she works with the same assistant from her home office. Her move was motivated by a desire to be independent and her eagerness to lead a more informal life in surroundings of her own creation. She looks forward to going to work at 5 a.m., having lunch with her husband, and, perhaps, gardening in the afternoon.

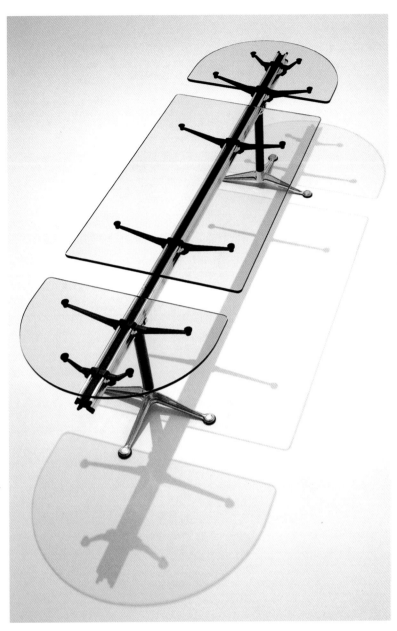

Jim Forrest is a partner in a large New York management consulting firm. The prospect of working at home some of the time became increasingly attractive as he began taking a greater interest in raising his three-year-old son. Recently it became practical for Jim to make the transition; on-line data services and high-speed telecommunications have made communicating from his home in Croton almost as easy as from his Park Avenue office. His income is sufficient to justify almost any office expense, and so he was able to replicate his office environment at home, including virtually all of the same equipment. Jim invested $100,000 in his lifestyle change but felt it was justified as long as his productivity didn't suffer. He still takes the train into Grand Central Station twice a week for lunches and client and partners' meetings but performs nearly all of his desk work from home. Jim has no plans to move from Westchester County and no plans to change careers.

These and other home office workers are changing the face of neighborhoods and affecting traffic patterns as flex-time schedules, two-parent child care arrangements, independent contracting, and the proliferation of personal computers help create new ways to work. No longer are American businesses and institutions strictly dependent on nine-to-five commuters. Increasingly, the two-income family, the spread of computer literacy and electronic telecommunications, the revival of family life, and the rise in neighborhood cohesion have come together to create a huge and growing number of home office breadwinners, as full-time, part-time, flex-time, and after-hours workers.

According to architect Travis Price, a home office worker in Takoma Park, Maryland, "mixed-use housing is not only the wave of the future but a necessity. Work at home allows neighborhoods to be used during the day instead of only as bedroom communities."

Your home office should be planned to meet your needs and to improve the quality of your work and productivity. This book is written for the millions of workers who spend or plan to spend a substantial part of their working lives in their home offices and want to make their environment as efficient and pleasant as possible.

As corporations decentralize and downsize their operations, an increasing number of highly paid executives, particularly in sales and marketing, are retreating to elegant and elaborate home offices, complete with all the trappings of their former executive suites. Herman Miller's classic lounge chair and ottoman, *opposite*, were designed by the legendary Charles Eames. This Herman Miller conference table, *above*, can also be used as a dining room table.

This grand entrance for a residence designed by Jim Williams in Huntsville, Alabama, includes a separate walkway to the left that is well lit and clearly delineated for business visitors.

CHAPTER I
PLANNING DECISIONS

While there are many approaches to planning a proper home office, they all seem to boil down to a few options: either you build or buy a new house that incorporates a home office; you add on to or renovate the house or apartment you already own; or you simply refurnish or redecorate part of a home or apartment you own or rent. If you are in business for yourself you will, of course, bear the entire cost of the project. If you work for someone else, you may also bear the entire cost, although some employers will pay for equipment they require you to use. The fact that employers often do not wish to bear the cost of home office construction has led many employees to turn in their 401(k) plans, their social security match, and their parking place for a contract to become a contingent worker, a consultant, and the freedom to make their own schedule, market their own fantasies, and plan and equip their own home office.

Perhaps the most difficult but critically important part of any planning program is predicting the future. If you are beginning a new business or planning to start one in the future, you may have only a vague idea of your needs. Under these circumstances it is essential that you postpone a large renovation until your second or third year in business, when you'll know better what you can afford, whether you'll need to make desk space for assistants or a partner to work with you, how often to expect visits by clients and colleagues, how much storage space you'll require, and the hundred other small matters that can help or hinder efficiency. There is no substitute for the experience you'll gain in the first year at home, forcing you to test assumptions before making expensive, irreversible decisions about your requirements.

For a full-time, professional, electronically sophisticated home office, it is important to think through the processes of your work, your comings and goings, electronic and paper storage, computer equipment and peripherals, telecommunications, and the relationship that you will have to your office when you are away from it—on the road, for instance, or during off-hours.

For those who will be using their home office part time, in the evenings and on weekends, meticulous planning may seem less important. Whatever the use, a carefully considered plan can be drawn that reflects both need and whim and provides a reliable means to estimate the cost of the project.

Fabric designer Jack Lenor Larsen built this extraordinary home studio and office as part of a 12,000-square-foot residence, "Longhouse." Situated on a 16-acre site of gardens and sand dunes, it was created in collaboration with architect Charles Forberg in East Hampton, New York.

This home office with five workstations is one of two "studios under the eaves" located in what Larsen calls "found space" in different wings of the house.

While in planning, Larsen learned about industrial designer Geoff Hollington's new line of homelike furniture for the office, called Relay, which Hollington characterizes as "designed to reflect the complex nature of creative work, which can be idiosyncratic, unplanned, and non-geometric." Working with John Berry of Herman Miller, the manufacturer of Relay, Larsen integrated space and furnishings together in the planning.

The following checklists may prove helpful as you plan your home office:

Home checklist
- Floor and wall space
- Flooring
- Walls
- Windows

- Heating, ventilation, air quality, and cooling (HVAC)
- Acoustics
- Electrical
- Illumination
- Plumbing

- Surfaces and seating
- Furniture
- Storage
- Telecommunications

- Privacy
- Security and safety

Furniture and equipment checklist
- Desks and surfaces
- Chairs
- File storage and shelving
- Ergonomics
- Computer hardware and peripherals
- Copiers and facsimile machines
- Telephones and telecommunication devices

Architect Thomas Tomsich's home office studio on Long Island Sound is detached from the main house. Interior spaces were carefully planned for the sloping site, with interior work spaces existing on two levels.

Home offices that are in constant use and that also accommodate more than one worker benefit from variations in floor and ceiling levels, multiple rooms, changes in floor covering, and other ways of delineating separate work areas. (For additional views of the Tomsich studio, see pages 74–77.)

Inventory

Knowing what you have to work with is essential. Your inventory includes those physical objects that must be placed, mounted, stored, displayed, and otherwise configured in your new space, including furniture, equipment, files, books, journals, and manuals. It also includes qualitative aspects such as privacy and safety.

As you develop a program you may decide to abandon furniture and files, buy new equipment, and otherwise significantly change the items on your inventory. The point is not to get everything right as you start, but to find a reasonable starting place for your plans.

In many home renovation construction projects, the largest cost category is for changes in the work. **Melinda Davidson** began building her office without a clearly defined scope-of-work agreement with her builder, and a series of minor disasters ensued. A careless measurement resulted in tearing out a closet. Another mistake meant using a jackhammer to change a footing. And so it went. In the end, miscalculations and changes of mind cost the Davidsons $1,100 they hadn't budgeted.

When **Jim Forrest** began preparing the functional program for his home office, he didn't worry about getting too organized at the outset. He simply began with whatever seemed important: he clipped magazine and newspaper articles relating to the look, feel, orientation, and capability of his ideal office. He made a scrapbook and prepared rough sketches and floor plans. He worked with an inexpensive two-dimensional CAD (computer-aided design) program on his computer to lay out furniture arrangements using existing rooms in his house, as well as hypothetical new spaces. And, of course, being a financial professional, he plotted alternate budgets for various office configurations and materials.

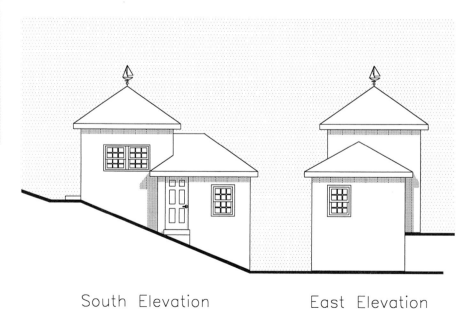

South Elevation   East Elevation

Home Alone: Basic Questions to Ask Yourself

Once you start planning your home office, you'll quickly become immersed in myriad details and decisions. To maintain a clear conception of the goals for your home office, you might want to keep in mind these basic questions as you plan:

- Can you organize your life to maintain or increase productivity from your home office?
- Why do you need (want) a home office?
- How much can you afford to spend on a home office project?
- Do you and/or your spouse plan to use the space for a full-time home occupation, for occasional or part-time work, or as a multiuse space?

Fundamental to your planning is choosing the space. Will you select an existing room, converting it with or without substantial alteration? Other options might include building a loft, raising the roof, enclosing a porch, or building an addition, either as an isolated project or as part of a larger home remodeling scheme.

Once designed and built, it may be too late to decorate without making adjustments. It is far better to think about finishes and surfaces, materials, furniture, and equipment as you plan. Carpeting requires a different kick molding from tile; window treatments depend on whether your windows open in, out, or up. The more you can settle before you start, the less likely you'll need to make costly changes while work is in progress.

Finally, consider your home office as either "dedicated" or "nondedicated" space. Dedicated space is set aside for your exclusive use as a home office and is not used for anything else. For a home business with a multiperson staff, dedicated space is nearly essential.

Space that is not dedicated—such as a spare bedroom that doubles as an office and a guest room—obviously works best as an office if the second use is only occasional. The reverse is also true. If you only require a home office occasionally, or if the time that you use it is highly discretionary, it may fit best in a nook off the living room or other semipublic area of the house.

One of the reasons people select their homes as a place to work is the opportunity to spend more time with their families. Dual income households with children in which both husband and wife have long daily commutes can create a scheduling nightmare, with little room to maneuver, little tolerance for a late meeting or a missed train, and scant flexibility to attend a special evening or a child's school play. With one or both adults in a family working from home, the dynamics of family life change dramatically: a chicken for dinner can be taken out of the freezer at 11 a.m.; a child who comes home after lunch with a runny nose can be tended to; a plumber's visit can be scheduled more readily; the family can enjoy a leisurely bike ride together through the neighborhood before dinner.

Jim Forrest suggests that you can dramatically increase your productivity when working from a home office if you observe these common sense rules:

- Keep regular office hours and consider dressing for work in the same clothes you would wear to a downtown office
- Close your door or otherwise separate yourself from your household during the workday except for breaks
- Keep the kids out of the office except when they are invited in
- Maintain your home office to the same degree of orderliness that you maintained your corporate office
- Plan a comfortable, attractive, appropriately lit, heated, cooled, ventilated, and furnished workplace
- Develop routines for bookkeeping, purchasing office supplies, and other overhead activities
- Find peace and quiet in your home office
- Move around, exercise, and vary movements to avoid stress and strain
- Maintain outside contacts for lunch or meetings that expand your specialty, professional standing, client base, or other advancement objectives

THE COMPLETE HOME OFFICE

The downside for many is the fear that they'll remain in their pajamas all day, indulge in their children's snack food and leftovers from the refrigerator, watch HBO movies, take the afternoon off to attend a son's football practice, and wind up out of work, in debt, overweight, and screwed up. The opposite is actually true. Home office workers often do not know when to quit and wind up working more hours than before—sometimes as much as 50 percent more.

Melinda Davidson averaged a forty-five-hour workweek in her job with a Fortune 500 company. Now, as her own boss, she averages fifty-five to sixty hours per week, yet it doesn't seem to her that she's putting in more time. Not having to commute frees up at least ten to fifteen hours each week, and she's glad to rechannel those extra hours into graphic design.

Surveys have shown that work habits at home are similar to those at the office. When commuting time is eliminated, along with time spent in meetings and office socializing, there are simply more hours in the day for home office workers.

Jim Forrest doesn't obey all of these rules all the time, especially the one about keeping the kids out—his little boy is very persistent. But generally he does practice what he preaches, and he hasn't suffered any loss of income since he moved into his home office.

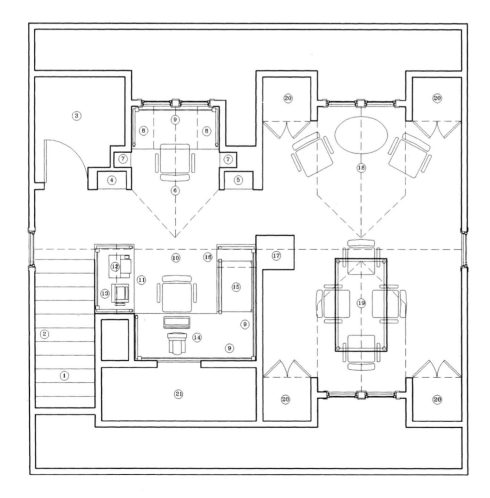

1. Stair
2. Gallery Wall
3. Coat Closet/General Storage
4. Bookshelves
5. Stereo Equipment/Bookshelves
6. Billing Area
7. Bookshelves
8. File Cabinet (below)
9. Pin-up Reference Board
10. Computer/Drafting Area
11. Reference Library (below)
12. Printer
13. Fax/telephone
14. CAD Workstation
15. Manual Drafting Station
16. File Cabinet (below)
17. Existing Brick Chimney
18. Waiting Area
19. Conference/Layout Table
20. Storage
21. Archives

By thinking through the placement of every piece of equipment, type of work space and kind of storage requirement in advance, problems can be anticipated long before construction begins. Attic floor plan, *left*, and exterior, *opposite*, of the home studio and office of architect Thomas Quarticelli in Wethersfield, Connecticut.

Looking at the Space in Your Home

Any place you select will have pluses and minuses, but some spaces are more appropriate for home offices than others. You may be thinking about converting your attic, spare bedroom, storage room, garage, porch, or basement. How do you fit every requirement and desire into an existing space, an available budget, and schedule without forgetting something and without making mistakes?

There are several ways to approach the issues but only a few ways to solve the problem. Before you decide what should go into your home office, decide where it will be. Then move onto considerations relating to the physical arrangement of the space and the installation of infrastructure—lighting, cabling and other wiring, partition walls, etc. These are important whether you are moving into an existing room in your house or building a new space. You may wish to leave all of the design to your architect/designer/builder team or you may wish to do it all yourself. Most people do some themselves, leaving that which requires expertise to the experts.

Attic

That space above your head is so near and yet so far. What may seem the simplest and least expensive conversion may turn out to be the toughest. The slope of the roof and its

The Quarticelli home studio and office under construction, *opposite*, and complete, *above* and *right*. For attic offices and studios, it is essential that all furniture and equipment that is planned for the space be measured to ensure adequate access. Headway and turning room are often extremely tight on attic stairs, which also may require reconstruction to meet building code requirements.

height above the attic floor are the critical variables in judging the suitability of an attic for conversion. Is the center beam high enough to meet code requirements (usually seven feet)? The floor area beneath the center beam where you have a seven-foot clearance is the usable space for your office (although you can use the space of descending height for storage).

Melinda Davidson and her husband thought their attic seemed ideal for her home office—until a friend who'd also built a home office in her attic pointed out potential problems:

• **Ceiling height:** Melinda's attic ceiling height was quite low. Raising the roof or adding dormers was possible but very expensive. The roof beams in most houses literally hold your house together, and you cannot easily cut through beams to add dormers or make other alterations without making extensive compensating adjustments.

• **Light:** Most attics are dark. Cutting in windows or skylights along the roof is always possible but can pose installation problems; for example, special scaffolding may be required. Skylights are more expensive than windows and must be carefully installed to avoid leaks.

• **Access:** The thought of carrying a twenty-inch color monitor or a full-size copier up to an attic is daunting.

Attics may pose access problems for equipment and supply deliveries, visitors, and employees, and simply the time it takes to get to the front door from your office desk. Melinda found that it took a minute and a half to travel from her attic to the front door. Too long!

Building codes require that the steps to your home office meet minimum standards in their rise and width, which will require floor space below into a convenient area. Installing spiral stairs, which require less floor space than a conventional staircase yet still meet building code, may not be practical for moving furniture and equipment in and out.

• **Heating, Ventilation, Air Quality, and Cooling (HVAC):** Attics are often stuffy (no vents) and are too hot or too cold most of the time. Melinda's house had a forced air heating system with adequate capacity so she could run ducts into the attic for heating and cooling but would probably need to add insulation in the ceiling. Many houses already have insulation beneath the attic floor to retain heat and cool air in the house. However, given the space and expanse of surfaces in many attics, insulating, heating, and cooling this kind of home office may be more expensive than you have planned for.

Clients enter the Quarticelli home studio through the front door and up a narrow stair to the attic. Photo *below* depicts completed attic studio with dormer. Elevation drawing, *right*.

Some home offices are carved out of virtually no space at all. This bedroom niche office was designed by New York designer Freya Block for a Park Avenue psychotherapist, who sees patients in the living room.

Bedroom

If an attic is the most difficult conversion for a home office, a bedroom may be the easiest. Although people with children at home may not have a bedroom to spare, home office workers without children at home are more likely to have a bedroom available than any other room.

Unlike the difficulties encountered in attics, heating and cooling a bedroom is not a problem, nor is moving equipment in and out, having natural light, getting to the front door or to a bathroom, or meeting code requirements if you require a building permit in a remodeling project.

The downside to a spare bedroom, particularly if it is located where the other bedrooms are, is that its access by business visitors is restricted to times when that part of the house is not in use. If a strict separation between work life and home life is essential to your productivity, then a spare bedroom may not be a good choice for your home office.

Greg Simpson wanted to move out of his dining room, which had been serving as a makeshift home office, and the bedroom seemed the likeliest place. It didn't last. He soon realized that the place where you sleep should be a refuge from work. Working and sleeping in the same room created a feeling of never-ending work for Greg, intruding into a place where peace and quiet are paramount.

New York designer Alvin Schneider built this closet low-tech (no computer) office for a professional organizer who has written a book and lectures on organizing one's life. The office looks like an armoire when closed, a fully functional home office when open. There is a twin unit on the other side for the client's husband.

Storage Room or Closet

For full-time office workers, a storage room or closet may not be large enough; for others, these spaces can be converted into splendid offices. If your storeroom has an outside wall, it may be possible to install a window or outside entry.

Such extremely compact arrangements for a single-worker office—sometimes called "pocket offices"—can be very satisfactory. One advantage is that everything is within easy reach. The drawback, of course, is that you will only have room for the bare essentials. You will also need to provide such necessities as electrical outlets, heating and cooling, and lighting. The pocket office is particularly well-suited for apartment dwellers and those who cannot dedicate a whole room to office use. If properly planned, a pocket office does not need to be claustrophobic or dark. One approach to building a home office in a closet is to contact a company that provides built-ins for closets, such as California Closet Company. A closet office can be designed to provide desk space and storage within the closet but permit you to sit outside the closet itself, where there is more light and air circulation.

Garage

Newer houses sometimes have huge garages with room for not only a home office but a mid-sized home-based corporation. With builders ever-striving to create magnificent curb appeal among suburban residences, the American garage has ceased to exist as a shelter for a car but instead has evolved into an important part of the house itself. Some garages have shuttered windows and roof dormers and space that can be built into two stories.

Before World War II, garages were often out back, on the far side of the backyard facing an alley—where horses were kept when garages were called stables and the smell needed to be kept away from the house. These detached garages pose a different set of problems from the modern attached garages that are larger and are part of the house itself. Detached garages, like gardener's sheds, barns, and other old-fashioned outbuildings, can be converted into great office space, but the scale of these projects is different from the conversion of an attached garage of a house of more recent vintage.

When **Elizabeth Haskell** was still working downtown and needed only an occasional home office, she tried using part of the detached garage in back of her house. Although she walled off the office space from the car area, the faint smell of automobile exhaust persisted. The odor wasn't terrible; it was more a source of worry. What will this do to my health? Will it irritate clients and cause me to lose accounts? She decided to construct a separate building to house her home office.

Garages are one of the least expensive solutions for creating a spacious, light-filled, and accessible home office that is both out of the way and convenient. A major drawback to converting your garage is providing HVAC (heating, ventilation, air quality, and cooling); a substantial new or auxiliary heating and cooling system as well as complete insulation may be required.

Obviously, using your garage for a home office will leave your car out in the cold. While southerners might add a carport, workers in northern climes must consider the trade-off of a garage conversion with the attendant inconvenience of scraping snow and ice off their car after each winter storm.

Porch

Porches, Florida rooms, sunrooms, and other summery rooms of a pre-air-conditioned age often make excellent home offices but are hard to give up. Anyone who has spent a cool summer evening on a screened porch would find it difficult to use that space for other, more practical purposes like housing the PC and fax machine.

Nevertheless, a porch—front, side, or rear—can become a very satisfactory office at home, providing easy access and a garden view. Another advantage is that renovating porches, like garages, is far less invasive than renovating attics and other interior rooms. If you have a temporary set-up now, you can probably continue your work without an interim move. For other construction projects, you may encounter weeks, even months, of disruption.

A garage can be a convenient location for your home office if you are willing to forgo a place for your car and can develop a practical and economical method to heat and cool the space. This office, designed by architect Donald Eurich, was converted from an 1875 carriage house, which was formerly used as a car garage, woodworking shop, and motorcycle repair shop.

Floor plan includes a large open studio (left) and a guest apartment for visiting associates and consultants (right). The loft space (above) serves as a personal office area, with existing basement (not shown) for a model-making shop. The area of these spaces is 1,300 square feet, enough to accommodate a staff of six to eight people.

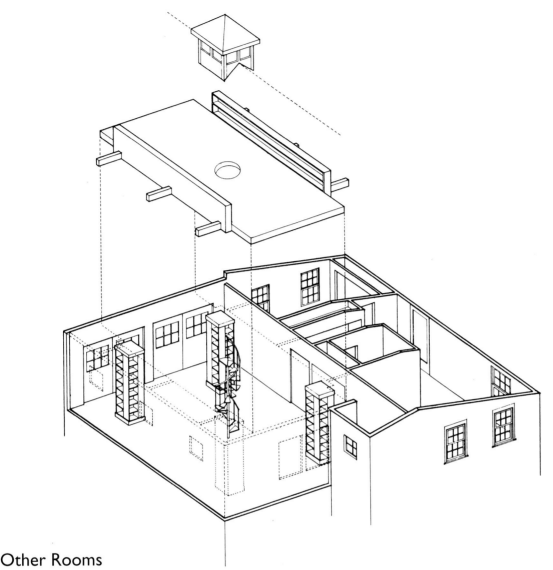

Other Rooms

Apartment dwellers, people who live alone, people who live in small houses, and those who need a home office only part of the time may be able to create satisfactory work space in a room that also serves another purpose, for example, a living room or dining room.

In fact, a home office tucked into an alcove off a living room or behind pocket doors in a dining room may be ideal because these rooms function well for greeting visitors or for conferences. Dens, family rooms, and other ancillary recreational areas can also work, but conflicts with other family members are likely to arise at least some of the time.

Greg Simpson realized he had made a bad decision in moving his office to his bedroom. The question was, where to try next? The only other possibility was the living room, which he quickly ruled out. The living room was his place to unwind, relax, be lazy—and not even think about work. Why had he moved out of the kitchen? he wondered. Thinking back, it was because he'd gotten tired of hearing comments from his friends, his girlfriend, and his mother, who scolded, "Greg, get serious! This kitchen table setup is about as professional as a children's lemonade stand."

But he had gotten a lot of serious work done at the table. He loved cooking: the aromas of stews and roasts and curries had a calming effect on him and, he was convinced, helped him work better. So that was the answer. He'd remodel the kitchen—something he'd been planning to do anyway—and partition off a small but adequate space for an office. It would be out of the view of dinner guests, but stove, oven, and cutting board would be within six steps of his desk. It worked.

Shoppe at 2210

As hordes of people are bringing their offices home, a few San Diego pioneers are moving home to office, a return to the home-over-the-shop European tradition that was also prevalent in American cities until World War II.

Architect Dale Naegle designed and developed shopkeeper homes that combine home with either office or retail store. For retailers who do not have the option of working at home, this concept offers all the advantages of home and office combinations as well as a 31-year, straight-line depreciation on 60 percent of the building. Front street facade, *opposite*, showing business below and home above; street-level clothing store, *right*; elevation, and second-floor living area, *below*.

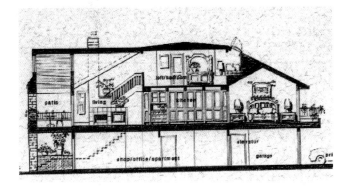

Basement

To take full advantage of these features, you must have a house with a full basement with plenty of headroom, some natural light, and, preferably, access to the street. Among the advantages of a basement office:

- easy access and sometimes a separate entrance
- may not require insulation, or new or modified heating and cooling
- enough space
- removed from the noise, traffic, and commotion of the household
- can be used late or early without disturbing others in the household
- is often a place that others won't want to be if they're not working
- may have some natural light but not enough to cause glare problems with computer displays
- good storage
- easy to secure against burglaries when you are away

   The problems with basements are dampness (which can be corrected mechanically), flooding (sump pumps, proper drainage and gutter system, and a location not prone to flooding are all helpful), no natural light (a substantial problem for people who believe they must have a window and view to the outside), ceiling height, and decor, which is the easiest of all the potential problems to correct.

Bonus Rooms

Builders have become increasingly interested in the work-at-home phenomenon. Beginning in the late 1970s, new medium-to-large houses began to feature unfinished "bonus" rooms—typically in the basement or off a garage—that could be completed by the builder or owner to a custom specification. More recently, the fashion has turned to "flexible" homes that include suites of rooms with separate entrances and bathrooms for home offices, rental apartments, in-law suites, or caregiver's quarters for the elderly. The concept was pioneered by southern California architect Aram Bassenian, who stresses the advantages of a flexible design: "We buy a house thinking we are going to live there forever, yet most of us move within five years. One of the reasons people move is that their needs change....The intent is to minimize the impact of remodeling by prepping a house for change."

   There are obvious cost advantages in developing a home office out of space designed to be apart from the rest of the structure. It also makes sense if you think you'll eventually outgrow your home office, retire, or use it for a separate living space within the dwelling.

   Elizabeth Haskell and her husband have decided that if they leave Nashville when they retire, they'll build a new house with a "bonus room," which they may use for a study, library, or recreation room. But they're really including it as a "safety valve," in case one or both of them doesn't really cotton to retirement and needs an office.

Basement offices are often spacious, incorporating several rooms, and often have bathrooms. This office of designer Joan Ravasy and her husband in Lebanon, New Jersey, has its own front entrance and is decorated in basic black and white. A wall of custom cabinetry, *left*, houses files and audio-visual equipment. The office has ample space for office equipment, including fax, phone, and a **CAD** system.

Access is critical in planning a basement office, while the availability of natural light may be a luxury that cannot be easily accommodated, *below*. Joan Ravasy reaches her home office by descending a circular stair, requiring very little space, *left*. She also has a small but adequate window at ceiling height to let in a little natural light, *opposite*, in addition to ceiling track lights for ambient illumination.

Architect Ray Townsley of Huntsville, Alabama, designed his own home with carefully delineated zones to permit the comings and goings of his busy design practice without interference with his family life.

Townsley expanded his one-story white Cape Cod house with a two-story addition many years ago, later adding an office to house his growing design practice. "Combining home and office meant that I needed to analyze my finances in a new way," said Townsley. The hub of the addition is a two-story atrium connecting the studio and the main residence. The ramp at right leads to driveway.

Privacy

To make an intelligent decision regarding the right room for your office, you need to consider the issue of privacy. Privacy for your home office means separating your life from your work in such a manner that your work gets done but does not unnecessarily interfere with family life. For some, working in the midst of everything else is both desirable and perhaps the only alternative. Mothers or fathers with an infant at home and no other child care may wish to be positioned so that work can be accomplished in snatches, between feedings and in captured moments of quiet throughout the day and evening. But most of us not similarly situated will want to design our home office for sufficient, if not complete, privacy. A psychiatrist who sees patients at her home office, for example, certainly does not want any interruptions, distractions, or evidence of domesticity when her patients are present.

But different kinds of workers require different kinds of spaces. Do you wish to create a flexible space for the whole family to use as needed or a private space for your use only? Do you and your spouse wish to share a single desk, or do you want to create two workstations with two desks, or do you prefer to build separate work areas? Final decisions about these matters may not be possible at first, but eventually you will have to make choices. Too much space in your home office will be inefficient, wasteful, and unnecessarily expensive. Too little will be regrettable.

Most dwellings and residential neighborhoods were not designed to provide appropriate privacy for office work. In modern, post–World War II houses, family rooms are often open, while closed, private spaces such as bedrooms are often located in the wrong place for use as an office. If clients come to your office for a meeting, will you take them through the house to the bedroom area—where your teenage daughter is still asleep or your visiting father-in-law is on his way to the bathroom—or will you meet in the family room amid your son's train set and grandma's knitting? Are you likely to disturb your family, talking on the phone at 4 a.m. to a colleague in Singapore?

If you work full time in your home office, you probably will want to be physically removed, at least most of the time, from the comings and goings of your family. A single person using a second bedroom in an apartment will not encounter these problems.

Jim Forrest wanted to separate his home office from the rest of his house but still make it accessible, especially for his young son's visits. He decided to make a separate entrance for it from the foyer adjoining the porte cochère. A visitor can enter the foyer and knock on the office door. His son knows he can just twist the knob and walk in—during his regular afternoon visiting time.

Home Office Strategy: Separating Home from Office

There was at least one issue that I failed to anticipate when planning my home office. For years I had suffered from sinus problems that almost completely obliterated my sense of smell. Soon after completing my home office, I underwent surgery that alleviated most of the problem.

Each afternoon at about 4 p.m., preparation of our evening meal commences and, even with the windows tightly shut, enticing aromas begin to waft into my office, located below and behind the kitchen. After some investigation I finally concluded that cooking odors were being sucked from the kitchen into our house's ventilation system and were drifting down to my office.

The problem is often acute, especially on weekends when early morning sprints across my Macintosh keyboard are interrupted by the sweet smell of French toast being cooked on the stove by my wife, Lydia, and five-year-old Sam. While lawn mowers and air-raid sirens can also be distracting, I find odors from the kitchen a sure-fire way to dampen any further desire to work. By closing a vent in the kitchen and redirecting one in my office, the problem was solved easily.

Privacy Checklist

Consider your everyday and your occasional requirements:

- Do you go to work before the rest of the household is awake? Do you work after hours when others are sleeping?
- Do you have small children who need to be kept away from your work area?
- Do you require an appropriately businesslike setting for associate and client visits?
- Will you retain full-time, part-time, or occasional assistance in your office?
- Will your home office be located near a convenient and appropriate lavatory?

Outside the Office

All of your careful planning to create an office where clients and other visitors will feel welcome will be in vain if you make them run an obstacle course trying to get from their car to your door.

In some neighborhoods, curbside parking is not a problem during weekday hours because most people are using their cars to commute to work. Other neighborhoods permit no curbside parking and require visitors to park in an area you provide. In any event, home office workers who expect visitors—clients, temporary employees, and delivery, sales, or repair people—should consider street profile and office access as part of their planning.

As you plan for your home office, obtain a plat of your property so that you or whomever is helping you can locate the exact boundaries. Think about ways that you can both separate and integrate your home "life" with your home "work."

To delineate outdoor spaces around your home, you may use gates or doors, stairs, patios, decks, porches, drives, walkways, fences, walls, hedges, shrubs, trees, and flower beds. Think about seasonal differences and carefully consider drainage. Evergreen shrubs and hedges that retain their leaves in winter are a good choice for northern climates. If your program requires extensive planning, consult a landscaping service or landscape architect. Landscaping services often provide a free plan if you engage them for materials and installation. Some landscape architects also work as contractors, while others provide consulting and design services for a fixed fee or hourly rate.

Conference area, *opposite*, and drafting room, *above*. **While a significant number of architects and interior and graphic designers have traditionally worked from home, an increasing number of sales and marketing executives, analysts, programmers, and other professionals are now home workers, but require less space than designers.**

The Great Outdoors

Some of the questions you should consider in planning the outside approach and entrance to your office include:

- Where will the visitor park?
- How will the visitor get from car to home office?
- Can outdoor living areas—children's play equipment, picnic table, pool, etc.—be screened from the approach?
- Is an outside entrance possible?
- If you have an outside entrance, can hand truck deliveries reach your home office entrance? Do you have access for wheelchairs? (While the Americans with Disabilities Act does not specifically require handicap access for homes, this is an important consideration for many people planning home offices.)
- Is the approach—from car to entrance—safe?
- Can you mark the approach in a manner that makes the way clear to a first-time visitor?
- Will you need to light the way for late-in-the-day winter or night callers?
- Will additions or changes to your present landscape require more time or money to maintain?

57

Home Office Strategy: Visit to a Small Office

Chevy Chase, Maryland—Occasionally, important visitors will make their way to my office. A client from Japan, whom I had not met before in person, arrived one spring morning by taxi with his translator. Since I suspected that there were not many home offices in Japan, it was particularly important that I present my working situation as professionally as possible.

From the driveway, the translator recognized the "Studio Entrance" sign which hung inconspicuously on the gate to the right of the front door. Entering this gate, my visitors walked across a terrace to an identical sign and through an identical gate. They descended stairs that led them to the entrance to my office. From my desk, I could see them arriving and greeted them at the door.

My home office was built as an addition behind an above-ground basement on a sloping lot. On the side away from the front entrance to the office is another stair leading to a deck, which was built over the office roof and which connects with a family room and kitchen. Within a relatively small space, home and office life are kept apart.

Plantings around the office were kept simple and functional. The ground cover requires no maintenance, and the dogwood trees positioned in front of each of the two windows help diffuse sunlight into the office.

I planned my home office first with rough sketches and then more precisely on my Macintosh computer. I consulted with a contractor, who helped me work through the various technical issues involved with grafting an addition onto an existing home. The most extensive planning related to landscaping and access issues, rather than construction of the home office itself.

If I had to do the project over I would probably make my office somewhat larger, although I have had no significant problems since its completion.

The author's approach and entrance to his home office were carefully planned to be harmonious with the rest of the house, to comply with zoning, and to make clients feel welcome, making it easy for them to get from their car to the office door.

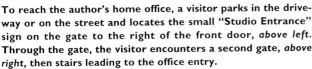

To reach the author's home office, a visitor parks in the driveway or on the street and locates the small "Studio Entrance" sign on the gate to the right of the front door, *above left*. Through the gate, the visitor encounters a second gate, *above right*, then stairs leading to the office entry.

Zoning and Permits

Let's say that you've decided to remodel a spare bedroom, add a separate entrance, and use it for your home office. The first thing you have to do is get the blessing of your local government.

Zoning Ordinances

Bill Toner, formerly a researcher for the American Society of Planning Officials, has suggested that for most communities, the regulation of home occupations has been a knotty problem, mainly because there are so many different kinds of businesses. In the main, communities that regulate home offices do so either to curtail high-volume or high-traffic activities.

In general, a home office zoning ordinance contains at least some of the following provisions:

• Only family members residing on the premises may

be engaged in the business. (Some jurisdictions state that no more than one or two persons other than a family member may be employed.)

• The use of the dwelling for the home occupation should be clearly incidental and subordinate to its use for residential purposes.

• There can be no change in the outside appearance, other than a small sign not exceeding one square foot in area, nonilluminated, and mounted flat against the wall of the principal building. Some areas regulate the use of accessory buildings for home occupations.

• No traffic will be generated by such home occupations in greater volumes than would normally be expected in a residential neighborhood. Many ordinances also prohibit the use and parking of a commercial vehicle on the premises.

• No equipment or process will be used in such home

occupation which creates noise, vibration, glare, fumes, or electrical interference detectable to the normal senses off the lot.

• Except for articles produced on the premises, no business inventory may be warehoused on the site.

• There shall be no use of utilities or community facilities beyond what is normal for residential purposes.

Toner's definition of a home occupation is "an accessory use of a dwelling unit for gainful employment involving the manufacture, provision, or sale of goods and/or services." Many ordinances do not require a permit but simply list (sometimes exhaustively) those occupations permitted and those forbidden in residential dwellings. In Glenview, Illinois, for example, dressmakers, music teachers, artists, dentists, lawyers, architects, realtors, insurance agents, ministers, and two dozen other occupations are permitted, while animal hospitals, barbershops, mortuaries, restaurants, stables, kennels, trailer renters, medical clinics, nursery schools, and repair shops are forbidden.

Most jurisdictions in metropolitan areas have some kind of ordinance on the books, although few have kept up with developments in technology and the expanding uses of home offices for traditional kinds of office work. The consequence is often a hodgepodge of antiquated, irrelevant rules.

Stairs terminate at the entrance to the author's home office. The large picture window and glass-paneled door permit natural light to reach entry area.

However, a little checking and applying some common sense are all that should be necessary. Modern home offices contemplated in this book are used primarily by workers whose occupations are sedentary, involving the shuffling of paper and the clicking sounds from a computer keyboard. If, however, you are a manufacturer working from a home office, it probably would be prudent to warehouse your inventory someplace other than your backyard. On the other hand, if your manufactured inventory fits into your garage or you receive supplies that are delivered by UPS or an express courier, you might be within the guidelines for your area.

When **Melinda Davidson** checked into her local zoning regulations concerning home-based businesses, she found that the ordinance prohibited the sale of goods on the premises except for "products of dressmaking, hand-weaving, block-printing, the making of jewelry, pottery or musical instruments, by hand, or similar arts or handicrafts performed by a resident of the dwelling." Although she considered herself an artisan, an electronic one, she didn't know whether she could sell her work product—graphic design—from her home. Her zoning director assured her that her works fell within the exemption.

The critical test will be the acceptance of your neighbors. If they begin to complain about too much noise, too many cars parked on the street, deliveries by large trucks, or a large neon sign posted in your front yard, the law may come to stalk your home-based business. Because each neighborhood is different,

Home offices that involve extensive construction usually require careful planning, including the close integration of office and residence to the site. For the author's home office project, the exterior stairs, rails, and outdoor seating areas were organized for twin purposes: the roof of the office serves as a deck adjacent to a family room and kitchen. The stair, *above*, leading from the deck, is one of four approaches to the home office.

sweeping generalizations can be only marginally useful. Before spending money on a big remodeling job, simply call your zoning board or planning department and ask for a copy of your jurisdiction's ordinance, or look it up at your local library. You might also try to learn how strictly your local government enforces the ordinance. Many places, particularly those that do not require a permit, do not enforce home occupation ordinances unless someone complains.

Building Permits

Virtually every jurisdiction in the United States and Canada has building codes and requires a permit to build, add to, or substantially alter your residence. Most home offices are planned so that they can also be used as a study, spare bed-

room, sewing room, or playroom. If you sell your residence at some later time, the new owners may use the space in a manner different from the way you did.

To protect your investment, it is wise to plan your home office to standards appropriate for a bedroom or living area, providing sufficient access and egress, headroom, ventilation, natural light, electrical outlets, insulation, and other variables to meet your jurisdiction's building code requirements. Keep in mind that a home office is not located in a commercial building and will not (nor should not) meet standards established for commercial spaces, such as fire exits, fireproof stairwells, elevators, and the like.

If you are adding to your existing space with a bump-out, a full addition, or a separate structure, a building per-

The author's two-room home office has stations for two workers, although a visiting worker can set up a laptop on the island work table. The computer monitors are suspended beneath a shelf to free a work space below. Book shelves line the opposite wall.

The view from the author's home office. Substantial light and air come through this large window, which opens either from the side (like a door) or at the top.

The direction the window faces, the foliage on the site, the time of day, time of year, weather, and the part of the country where you live are all factors in the amount and kind of light that filters into your home office.

mit and periodic visits by a building inspector will be a likely requirement. In general, projects that add space to, or add load-bearing walls in, a house will be supervised by an architect, designer, and/or a building contractor, each of whom has experience in dealing with these matters. Do not be surprised if they decline to designate this new space as a home office on the plans, which may or may not pass the scrutiny of your jurisdiction's building department. A study, bedroom, or playroom may be the more appropriate designation given the building codes, and will be inspected accordingly.

Home Office Strategy: Permits and Registration

My home office in Chevy Chase, Maryland, required no special permit or registration when I completed construction in 1991. The county regulations concerning home occupations indicated that I had a "no impact" home occupation, defined as having five or fewer client visits per week, no employees other than family members who reside on the property at least 220 days per year, and floor space devoted to occupational purposes not exceeding 33 percent of the total floor area of my dwelling unit. Myriad other requirements relating to parking and prohibiting equipment that created noise, vibration, fumes, odors, and electric or electronic interference detectable beyond my lot line were also described in exacting detail.

Two years later, I decided to engage one nonresident assistant, which changed my status from "no impact" to "registered" and required me to register my home office with the county. A *Registered Home Occupation* permitted (only) one additional worker, but up to a maximum of twenty client visits per week (but no more than five per day), excluding deliveries and the comings and goings of an assistant or "business associate."

Other questions on the registration application requested verification of the gross square footage of space for business use, total square footage of the dwelling, a legal description of the property, and an explanation of the proposed use of the intended occupancy.

After wading through the paperwork it occurred to me that registration protected me as much as my neighbors. Before registering, I had not known the specifics of the county's requirements and always had a vague worry that too many deliveries or client visits would trigger a complaint from my neighbors, with the home office police swooping down to curtail the activities at the back of my house. It is reassuring to know that the local government considers my home office to be perfectly legal, which in turn protects me from the possibility of an unwarranted grievance.

Financing

If you are self-employed in a home-based occupation, it may be useful to calculate the cost of alternatives before you decide to invest in a home office. For instance, your choices might include subletting a small office from another business; working from an "office suite," a commercially leased space that comes furnished and provides support services, such as a receptionist, copier, fax, and conference room; or leasing a small, stand-alone office that you furnish and equip yourself. In considering these alternatives, don't forget to factor in the cost of commuting and parking, expenses which don't exist at home.

None of these options may be right for you, but it is important to analyze them. If you establish a business at home, you may outgrow it and need to move. For reasons separate from your business, you may move your residence and require office space in the transition. Most important, you need to understand the costs associated with alternative solutions so that you can create a realistic budget for your home office.

Your analysis can be highly detailed and complex or relatively simple, but you should establish a rationale for budgeting the costs associated with your business as distinct from your home. The cost of office space is 100 percent deductible on your income taxes if your entire income is derived from business activity located at your home office. Mortgage interest expense on your house is also deductible as a family expense. For the purposes of making a calculation, treat the cost of your office expenses as a separate business expense.

Costs and financing must be considered within the larger context of the ultimate purpose of the office. As an occasional workplace and sometime weekend retreat, the costs of constructing and furnishing a home office are no different from those associated with remodeling a bathroom or kitchen. For a home office that will house a viable, profitable, and long-term home-based business, cost justification is entirely different and must be weighed in the light of projected cash flow, staffing, and equipment utilization, as well as against other options. A major addition to your home could also prompt an increase in your property taxes, utility bills, or other costs.

Home Office Strategy: Costs

My home office was created as a retreat from the congestion, expense, and inconvenience of a commute into Washington, D.C. From 1971 to 1988 I maintained an office in the Dupont Circle area of the city, watching my rent increase from $2.25 per square foot per year to $20.00 per square foot per year, leasing between 1,200 and 3,000 square feet as my graphic design and publishing business required. With the advent of personal computers, my staffing requirements and the nature of my work began to change. The size of my staff went from an average of twelve to just four employees by 1989.

One of my goals in moving to a home office was to reduce expenses and gross sales substantially but leave my own compensation at about the same level. While my plan was difficult to ponder and execute, factoring the cost of office space was relativly easy.

By moving from center city to suburbs, from a high-prestige, premium-priced building to an office at home, and from the expensive 1980s into the more modest 1990s, my office rent could be reduced from $20 to $12 per square foot, assuming that I would soon need to build an addition onto my house. My need for space could also be reduced from 1,200 square feet (the size of my four-person office) to about 400 square feet (in both cases I used some additional off-site space for dead file storage). My 1988 office rent expense was $24,000 (1,200 square feet x $20). My 1989 office rent budget was $4,800 (400 square feet x $12). Since both leases were calculated as "triple net," all taxes, utilities, and other operating costs were passed along to me as extras rather than borne by the landlord.

In April 1989, I reduced my staff to one part-time worker (who worked from her home) and moved temporarily into my knotty pine basement recreation room. After settling in, taking stock of my needs, and making many adjustments to my business activities to fit these new circumstances, my wife and I began to plan the construction of a home office together with a deck and landscaping project. From start to finish, the costs associated with the home office part of the project were kept completely separate from home- and site-related costs.

Using $4,800 per year as my budget, I calculated an allowance to build an addition based on a 7 percent, fifteen-year loan (first as a home equity loan and later, as rates declined, as part of a refinanced first trust). My $400-per-month budget purchased $45,000 in home improvements for an office, a sum that proved adequate for construction, finishing, and furniture.

How Much Does It Cost?

There are a number of questions you need to consider when factoring costs:

- How much can you afford to spend on a home office project, both now and later? The cost of the space, the furniture, and the tools of your trade must each be evaluated as either an expense or investment.

- If you build an addition or renovate a room, will your house increase in value by the amount you spend (plus interest lost from savings or incurred by borrowing)?

- Can you expand your business or improve your position by having a greater amount of space, or by having a more convenient, pleasant, and efficient office in which to work?

- What is that worth in real money? Part of your program for your new home office is the rationale for spending the money to create it. While exact calculations are impossible, you should have a feel for what is prudent.

Elizabeth Gillin's offices for her interior design practice are well integrated into her New Jersey home, yet are organized to be completely functional. Spaces that are used strictly for work are tucked away while areas for meeting clients are more homelike and social.

The costs and financing of your home office are, of course, related to the length of time you will use the office. It's an important factor in planning a budget, and more so if you undertake construction. Your direct, out-of-pocket costs in building and setting up a home office may or may not be tax deductible, which will also have a bearing on your budget.

Elizabeth Haskell and her husband (who teaches at Vanderbilt University) refinanced the first mortgage on their house to pay for construction of a home office, furniture, landscaping, and a new driveway; they budgeted a total of $51,000. Elizabeth will pay $528 a month for twelve years, the length of time that she expects to use her 900-square-foot home office. This amount is substantially less than the $800 per month she was paying to the partnership for the 750 square feet that she and her bookkeeping assistant occupied (including her portion of common areas) in a commercial Nashville office building.

Elizabeth planned her home office so that it would serve as the base for earning a comfortable living from a mature accounting practice. She felt certain that her accounts would remain stable, and so she did not allow for growth. She is amortizing the cost so that mortgage payments will end about the time she plans to retire.

As an accountant, Elizabeth knew that the $51,000 cost of her home office addition would not necessarily increase the value of her house if circumstances forced her to sell. She considered the prospect of selling before her retirement to be remote and the risks of faltering in her established practice to be slight.

For others in similar circumstances, these calculations are critical. For businesses and professional practices that are new or fragile, construction projects should be planned so that the space is suitable for other potential purposes and that the neighborhood can sustain the value added to the house if it is sold before the cost of the addition is amortized.

Calculating furniture costs is more subjective. **Jim Forrest** advised his brother-in-law, who also has a home office—and chronic lower-back pain—to buy a $400 ergonomic chair with substantial lumbar support. Jim feels that the chair may be less expensive than the medical bills associated with back problems. **Greg Simpson**, on the other hand, scoffed at the idea of spending the money for a chair with good support and continued to use one of his dining table chairs for his evening work. When he started getting backaches that affected his basketball games and workouts, he relented and persuaded his boss to let him take home one of the fancy chairs from headquarters.

Attractive, comfortable furniture is important not only for your health but also for your attitude. The more your office fits your home office goals, the more comfortable you'll be spending one, two, or three thousand hours there a year.

The cost efficiencies of your equipment and software are even more subjective and particular to your work, but also easier to calculate. You know now, or will know soon, which features at what price are most appropriate for your home office setup.

After sifting through all of these issues, you still will need to determine how much you can afford to spend or borrow for your home office, the categories of expense, and the time span over which the expenditures will be made or amortized. Many of the questions posed here will be unanswerable at first, but at least one question will be fundamental to your home office project: can you save money with a home office, and if not, is the cost justified for the convenience, productivity gain, or stress reduction?

For **Melinda Davidson**, moving from corporate office to home office generated other savings: child care; fuel, car maintenance, parking and bus or train fare; maintaining a professional wardrobe, including dry cleaning; restaurant lunches; and incidental expenses such as magazines and newspapers, umbrellas, and mid-morning coffee.

All of these seemingly inconsequential expenses can add up to hundreds of dollars per year and are relatively easy to cut—or at least trim—from your home office budget.

The home offices Elizabeth Gillin of Westfield, New Jersey, designed by and for herself, use different parts of her house, blending working spaces into a residential decor. For client meetings, Gillin uses this sun-filled presentation room adjacent to her work areas. A partners desk allows ample space for both client and designer to lay out plans and colors. On pages 68–69, a cozy alcove is used as a creative workstation.

Tax Deductibility and the Home Office

Your home office will probably be deductible from your income taxes if you work full time and earn all of your income from your home office, i.e., if you are self-employed. If your situation is otherwise, the answer is complicated.

The Wisdom of Soliman

In 1993 the U.S. Supreme Court found in its *Soliman* decision that earlier lower courts' decisions relating to home office deductions had been too lenient, based on their interpretation of Section 280A of the Tax Reform Act passed by Congress in 1976.

Soliman applied only to taxpayers who claim their offices at home as their principal places of business. In its decision, the Supreme Court struck down tax court and circuit court rulings which said that Dr. Soliman—who shuttled between hospitals and spent two to three hours each day in his home office—used his home as his principal place of business. In its findings, the tax court noted that Soliman maintained patient records, reviewed medical information, billed patients, and performed other necessary duties essential to his work from home. It also found that the hospitals which employed Dr. Soliman did not provide him with office space. These conclusions followed recent decisions that were based on the importance of the business functions performed in the home office; the business necessity of maintaining an office at home; the expenditures incurred by the taxpayer in establishing a home office; and whether the space was also used for another purpose.

The reversal of *Soliman* was based, in part, on the Supreme Court's insistence that "the point where goods and services are delivered must be given great weight in determining the place where the most important functions are performed," declaring that "the point where services are rendered or goods delivered is a principal consideration in most cases." The court noted that Dr. Soliman did not see patients in his home but performed only administrative tasks there.

If you work from a home office but perform services elsewhere, you must support your deductions by showing that you perform most of the work that earns you most of your income from home. A violinist who performs at Lincoln Center three hours a week but practices thirty hours a week at home cannot deduct the room at home where she practices. A general contractor who prepares bids on jobs and bills his clients from home cannot claim a deduction; nor can a caterer who cooks at home but serves meals elsewhere deduct the costs of her kitchen.

Greg Simpson's accountant told him he could not deduct his apartment, or any part of it, as a home office for tax purposes. First, Greg did almost all of his income-producing work on the road, in face-to-face meetings with customers and prospects, which right away ruled out a tax deduction. Second, even if he did all his work at home, he would only be able to deduct the tiny area off his kitchen that he actually used for an office—maybe 8 or 10 percent of his apartment's area. Greg could, of course, deduct his other expenses—phone, courier, equipment amortization, and unreimbursed travel. Since he was a staff employee, not self-employed, he used the "Employee Business Expenses" tax form.

According to Ray and Lee Knight, professors of accounting at Middle Tennessee State University and experts on the *Soliman* decision, the court simply brought into compliance the intent of Congress to abolish the home office deductions of "frivolous, personal expenses related to rooms used only occasionally for business." Since Section 280A was written, lower courts had gradually widened the definition of allowable deductions to the point of inviting abuses. While a definitive rule about what is allowable is difficult to determine, the Knights have stated that "the taxpayer must now demonstrate that the business activities conducted in the home office are more important than those conducted elsewhere...and perhaps also that the taxpayer spends more time in the home office than at other locations."

© 1995 MELABEE M. MILLER

Gillin used architectural details such as door and window moldings to transform an uninteresting corner into a pleasant space for work or to meet with clients.

Insurance

One of the most complicated issues in preparing a home office strategy is liability and casualty protection for your home, your equipment and furniture, and visitors to your home office. Many insurance agents and companies have not adequately prepared for the work-at-home revolution and do not have useful advice or adequate coverage plans.

Only recently have several companies begun to provide general liability insurance coverage for damage or injury that you cause in someone else's home or office (or that someone else causes in yours), computer insurance, and endorsements on your homeowner's policy.

As a separate issue, health insurance for your family, a group plan if you have employees, worker's compensation insurance, disability, business interruption, malpractice, and errors and omissions insurance are all matters of possible concern to home-based businesses and may require investigation. Often you will need different insurance agents and carriers for these various policies.

Jim Forrest found that his homeowner's policy did not protect him from an accident that might occur when a business visitor came to his house. He did not have many business visitors—he met with most of them at his Manhattan office—but if damage or injury occurred relating directly to the financial consulting service that he provided, then he would need business property insurance and general liability insurance, which would also protect him when he was away from his home office on business. In addition, business property insurance can include coverage for costly and valuable computer and other equipment. Jim was willing to pay the $500 in yearly total premiums for the two types of insurance.

Full-time, part-time, or occasional use of your office space will be important determinants in the kind and amount of insurance you'll need. Obviously, recommendations from a knowledgeable and trustworthy insurance agent are essential. Given the number of options and limitations of each type of coverage, the cost of the coverage will in large measure dictate the kind and amount of insurance you carry.

CHAPTER 2
DESIGNING THE HOME OFFICE

I f you look at a broad sample of both homelike home offices and offices at home that look like commercial offices, you might well conclude that the choices for creating an "ideal" home office are ultimately rooted in how it will be called upon to function. While designers may be clever at hiding an office behind a screen or tucking one into a closet, the ultimate task is to create a place for accomplishing a job. Kitchens are now designed as efficient spaces where tasks are performed in safety and comfort and without wasted motion. Home offices are no different. An office in a home may also serve as a guest room or as a place to watch television. Or it might be a twenty-four-hour-a-day work facility for several people to produce an information product on a short schedule.

Architect Thomas Tomsich's studio on Long Island Sound has two levels—the working area above, with a high ceiling, and the conference area below. The scale of each level is appropriate for standing, moving around, and sitting.

According to Tomsich, siting the building on two levels and hugging the hillside was required for the structure to be more in scale with nearby structures and the adjacent salt marsh. This also allowed a nice transition between "working areas" within the structure—which are at the upper level with higher ceiling heights—and conference, display, and pin-up areas at the lower level.

Working with an Architect, Designer, or Contractor

Most people who build additions to their house hire professional help. Small projects can be handled by a competent builder without an architect. Some interior designers will also prepare plans for small extension projects. Whether you hire professional planning and design assistance or go it alone, the basic steps of the process should be carried out with great care and scrupulous attention to detail. In the most simple terms, consider your home office project as consisting of four parts:

- inventory, including equipment and furniture
- concept and programming, overall purpose and space requirements
- design and planning, location and arrangement of space
- implementation, in which you prepare the program, an architect or designer provides the design, and a builder carries out the project

For many projects, an interior designer or a builder's or general contractor's draftsman may be all the help you need, depending on your own skill and temperament, the amount of time you can devote to the project, and the size of your budget.

The best criteria for assessing a professional's work are the recommendations of people whose judgment you trust relating to matters of practicality, taste, cost, and reliability. It is also important to actually check references:

- Fully discuss with current or past clients the nature of their project, their satisfaction with the financial arrangements, the timeliness of the work, how changes were handled, the quality of the work, and their overall satisfaction with the relationship.
- Speak with clients who have worked with an architect, designer, or builder on a project that is one or two years old (have problems arisen? how were they handled?), as well as with clients now in the process of design and construction.

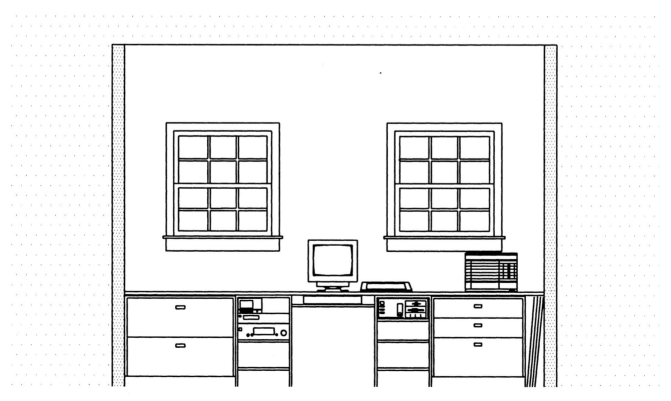

Depending on the particular circumstances, you may obtain references either before or after you have located a good candidate. In some cases, you may obtain a referral through a friend; you may also meet an architect or designer that you like, see their work, then obtain from them references for you to call. In any event, make sure that you speak to clients who can give you an objective report on the quality of their individual experience.

Contracts with building professionals range from standard forms developed by the American Institute of Architects to other standard or custom contracts, depending on local and individual practice. Whatever the format, it is essential that all work be spelled out in writing, including detailed specifications and plans for all agreements, costs, overhead, and (if you can get it included) profit. Typically, items such as carpeting and lighting are bid with an allowable budget. If you are in doubt or inexperienced with construction contracts, it is best to retain an architect or designer (with whom you will also sign a contract) to be your representative when negotiating a relationship with a contractor. Alternatively, consider retaining a lawyer familiar with construction to review the contract with your builder.

The Tomsich studio, *above*, sits approximately 75 feet from the main house. He uses it for his architectural work, and it includes a drafting table, CAD station, flat files, and general project files and reference materials.
Interior north elevation of the studio, upper level, *opposite*.

Bringing together your program and someone else's design takes time. For instance, you may find that parts of your program are impractical. While you know what your needs are, you may need substantial help from professionals to figure out the best, most practical way to meet them. Selecting a single person or firm to have overall responsibility for the project is a good idea. If you retain an architecture firm, it usually will take the lead and help you locate, and negotiate an agreement with, a contractor.

If you work directly with a contractor (without an architect) and use his draftsman, you may prefer to leave the space unfinished and hire an interior designer to help complete the details. Each home office project has its own set of requirements that will benefit from expert help. While experts do not necessarily provide the least expensive alternative, they often can provide cost-efficient solutions that pay off in the long run.

Keep in mind that the design of your home office is an essential, not frivolous, part of the process. Every home office is designed in some fashion (even Greg Simpson's dining table setup), but some arrangements make better use of space than others. Once dimensioned, arranged, and articulated with window and door openings and a basic electrical and HVAC plan, you and your design team should see how everything that you want or need fits into your office.

The design process will not move continuously in one direction, but will move back and forth from idea to program to plan to design, then back to you for review and comment, then back for revisions. New and better ideas will be generated along the way, some saving money, others costing more.

Form versus Function: Design Style

There is some confusion relating to the work and responsibility of various design professionals. While most architects design buildings and most interior designers decorate and furnish completed structures, there is also a great deal of crossover: most architects will also design complete interiors, and some interior designers will both design and manage small additions and other construction projects.

A designer may also provide the necessary architecture—such as partition walls or electrical work—while an architect may provide every service offered by a designer. For even a small project, an architect or a designer will probably be useful; for others, necessary. However, using both a designer and an architect at the same time for a small project can become a disaster if they disagree with one another, or duplicate work and generally get in each other's way.

In home office design, the divide is not between architects and interior designers but between those who stress function and those who focus on form. Traditionally, home office design was simply an extension of the decor of other rooms in the home. Carpeting and curtains, furniture and cabinetry were selected to blend in, continuing a distinctive design theme. However, this approach didn't always work well, because most homes are decorated in traditional styles, while most offices are modern. A clash of cultures was inevitable.

Starting from scratch—building home and office together at once—is ideal but requires considerable time and money. Most of us will have to make a fundamental choice about how integrated our home office will be with the rest of the house.

Integrating the decor is an obvious objective for home offices used for business meetings as well as family activities—a place to pay bills and prepare taxes, a place for children to do their homework or play computer games. For home offices that serve as full-time workplaces, located away from the traffic of the house, a functional decor becomes more important.

Manufacturers producing office furniture for the home grapple with the problem of creating ergonomically sound, convenient, and durable workstations, task chairs, file storage, and accessories that have the look and feel of an office yet are suitable for home use.

The availability of natural light can be a critical factor in creating a satisfactory setting for a home office, although the increasing use of computers mitigates against too much unregulated sunlight streaming into an office, which can create monitor glare. Shades and other window coverings help to control natural light, as can the reflective qualities of the wall and ceiling paint that one uses and the selection and placement of artificial lighting. Tomsich studio, *opposite* and *above*, employs windows, skylights, and artificial sources to flood the areas with light.

Melinda Davidson developed a personal style for her home office by combining a neutral, functional task chair, workstation, and storage system with distinctive moldings, drawer pulls and other hardware, an easy chair, artwork, and her personal collection of books. She believed that this approach followed the enduring traditions of the studio or atelier, home-based work space for architects, artists, and designers. The hallmark of this style is combining personal details with functional utility; a red velvet chair can look completely at home next to a guillotine paper cutter.

Color can also be used to blend contrasting home and office styles under one roof. Berkeley architect Sam Davis recommends stronger colors in home offices. "In commercial offices, where you try to please everyone who works there, the design has to be blander. In a home, it's possible to reflect one's personality more." Davis also suggests that in a home office you can use materials—fine fabrics, floor coverings, woods, and leathers, for example—that you would never use in a commercial setting because of high maintenance requirements or because they can't take the wear and tear of a commercial office.

Like **Greg Simpson**, you might consider also the color of your electronic equipment—computer, laser printer, fax, telephone, modem—when planning a room. These devices are usually light gray, beige, or black. By using these neutral colors for desks, file cabinets, carpeting, and walls, you can focus on accents—moldings, fabrics, art, books, objets d'art, desk accessories—to lend color to your office. Greg wanted the colors of his electronic equipment to blend with those of the fixtures and equipment in his kitchen, so he chose black.

Construction

Construction is a major undertaking and will disrupt your life even in the best of circumstances. Some people actually move out of their house altogether for the duration (which takes an average of two to three months for small projects and six or more months for big ones). One of the things **Melinda Davidson** did right in her planning was to hire a contractor who was already working in her neighborhood. Since he had more than one job underway on the same street, the contractor was able to save time and money by deploying his workers and subcontractors. For Melinda and her husband, this amounted to approximately a 5 percent savings.

Home remodeling will have enormous impact on you and your family through construction. Workers will be in and around your house from early morning to late afternoon. Things will go more smoothly if you try to maintain a friendly atmosphere on the site.

Carpenters are usually the ones who begin a job by framing out the room, and may continue to work on the site until near the end, when doors are hung and shelving is installed. **Jim Forrest** got to know his carpenters by name. He set out cold drinks at the end of hot days and left out the morning newspaper for people to read during lunch breaks. He made his telephone accessible to the foreman to check on deliveries. At the same time, he kept his son out of harm's way and tried to keep the mud off his carpet.

Contractors work on either a "cost-plus" (or time and materials) or a fixed-price contract. Many use a contract form developed by the American Institute of Architects, which covers both types of payments. You may also encounter a sophisticated cost analysis of work-in-process generated by construction software programs. Cost-plus contracts provide the contractor with a fixed rate for supervision and profit on all purchased services and materials. In addition, the contractor will estimate and submit a bid for the work his crew undertakes.

A fixed-price contract specifies the work to be accomplished and the price you will pay for that work. A fixed-price contract is often a misnomer because a project rarely comes in at the bid price. The problem arises when you change your orders. Any deviation from the original plans must be separately estimated and approved by you, along with the added cost, as work proceeds (for example, flitch plates or brackets may need to be added to provide more structural support in the framing). Change orders occur when site conditions differ from what was expected or when you change your mind. Extreme care must be taken with each discretionary change that you might consider since you are not in a particularly good negotiating position with the contractor over the cost of these changes. Outright mistakes by the contractor, of course, are not changes, and such expenses are borne by the contractor.

As you plan the launch of your home office addition, consider these important cost and logistical variables:

- Construction during inclement weather will take longer than under blue skies.
- During construction, you will be spending funds without the benefit of use. Consider the double expense if you will be paying rent to live and work elsewhere during the construction period.
- Construction creates dust, which can invade delicate electronic equipment. Keep your office equipment under wraps and well away from the construction activity.
- Coordination and scheduling are critical to a successful home office construction project. Failing to obtain the necessary financing and permits can delay a project start-up, which may push a contractor into scheduling conflicts or bad weather months. Try to anticipate potential scheduling problems.
- Gear your payment schedule to completion milestones. Negotiate a sufficiently large final payment that will give the contractor an incentive to complete the job in a timely fashion.
- Jobs are difficult to complete: a coatrack is back-ordered from a supplier; the paint on a rail is peeling almost before it is dry; a door sticks. Such problems plague every job and can only be satisfactorily settled with trust and goodwill (and a good contract) on both sides. Contractors depend on your recommendation to get more business. An unhappy client can drive a contractor from a neighborhood, while a happy client can often supply years of profitable work for a contractor who aims to please. Be reasonable in your requests.

Berkeley, California, architects Lisa Joyce and Sam Davis renovated the downstairs floor of a hillside house to be used as offices and also sleeping areas for guests; the area includes a fold-out bed and movable cabinets.

Getting Started: Design Considerations

Design, like the planning that precedes it, is perhaps best thought of as a set of separate but interdependent choices. Two tasks confront the designer: first, being aware of every important choice that must be made and, second, weighing the pros and cons involved in selecting the alternatives. The following guidelines should help on both counts as you develop a functional design program.

Site Plan

For new construction, consider how an addition or new structure will fit into its surroundings, how it will be oriented to the street, how convenient the driveway is to the entrance, how parking will be configured, and how the interior and exterior spaces will be integrated.

Floor Plan

Circulation patterns—interconnections between spaces—provide a sequence of visual experiences "that infuse a floor plan with the life and richness of good architecture," according to Sam Davis. The floor plan of most home offices is simple, a single rectangular room, demarking a doorway for access and places for windows and built-in furniture. Unlike rooms that change infrequently, work space should be more flexible and should accommodate such changes as an additional worker, new equipment, and expanding storage capacity.

The arrangement of furniture—both built-ins and stand-alone pieces—is critical. With space almost always at a premium, efficient furniture placement is critical.

Massing, Proportion, and Scale

As you review the plans of an architect or designer, keep in mind aesthetic considerations that make a place seem warm and inviting, sensible, appropriate, and even beautiful. With a floor plan, you can only gain a sense of the flat, horizontal surfaces of a room or a house. Massing, proportion, and scale provide the forms that grow out of a plan. Use your common sense as you walk through the space that will be your home office, assuming that it is already built. If you are planning to build new space, lay out the floor area with tape or string and place cartons the size of various furniture pieces in the space to provide necessary scale. Think carefully about how you will use the space:

Desk, *below,* and seating areas, *opposite,* at the Berkeley, California, home office of an academic couple. The areas are divided by a Japanese screen that helps to provide interesting and functional niches within wide open spaces for conversation and as a living room for overnight visitors.

- Is it too narrow to move around?
- Will there be room enough to position both your laser printer and your fax machine within arm's reach of your chair?
- Can you reach a telephone easily from anywhere in the office? A standing or sitting man or woman is the standard by which we evaluate the scale of a piece of furniture, a doorway, a ceiling height, or a whole room.

Character and Expression

Giving a space character and expression is often the baili-wick of an interior designer, who suggests, organizes, and directs the selecting and placing of furniture. The design-er also chooses wall and ceiling colors, carpeting, and window treatments. Honest, simple solutions are best for a home office. Too much color, too many frills, or too much eccentricity may grow tiresome if you are not dead certain of your own taste.

Office surroundings require some flexibility—you need to be able to move furniture, non-built-in desks and surfaces, and lighting, for example, on short notice. Some home offices are more home than office, while others strive to create as businesslike a setting as you would find in an insurance office in a downtown office building.

Jim Forrest had an idea. He would reserve a small part of the home office he was planning—say, a six-by-eight-foot corner space—for a play area when his three-year-old son, Jimmy, came to visit. Jim remembered the pictures of John F. Kennedy, Jr., at the same age, crawling around the Oval Office, and that had not kept JFK from running the country.

The kiddie corner was an instant hit. A little too pop-ular, in fact. Jimmy wanted to spend three or four hours each afternoon with his dad. Jim Sr. decided after a week of part-time productivity to shift this special father-and-son area to a corner of the family room. Now he meets his son there for lunch and plays with him in the office corner for an hour in the mid-afternoon.

While many home office workers depend on a computer, fax machine, and other equipment to perform their work, others simply need a place to read their mail, pay their bills, and make phone calls. It may be set up to look like an office, such as these areas designed by Sally Groth. Alternatively, studies, libraries, dens, family rooms, porches, hallways, and other home retreats can provide a space for a desk and storage that simply extends a private or social setting into a working space.

Lighting

Lighting is one of the most important design decisions you will make. Think about the type, quality, intensity, and placement of lighting you will need, and about both natural and artificial light for task and ambient illumination. Consider all of the other places where light will be needed: above a bookshelf and over your laser printer, off a wall where a picture is hung, in a closet or foyer, and, at night, at a doorway, an entrance, or near a gate. Lighting should be mixed among sources, both direct and indirect, task and ambient.

Those of us who spend a large part of our working day in front of a computer monitor will find that a low-level mix of natural and artificial light, with some bright spots for writing or other work requiring more light, is best.

In general, the ambient light level in your office should be similar to the light from your computer display. A footcandle is a measurement of the illumination of one candle falling on an object one foot away, while wattage is the amount of light emanating from a source. The recommended illuminance (that is, the light level that actually reaches the area to be lit) for writing and average reading materials at your desk is 50–100 footcandles. In a room that is dimmed for computer work, perhaps only twenty-five footcandles of illumination are needed, but the level varies greatly by personal preference.

A lighting contractor or personnel in a good lamp store should be consulted before selecting fixtures. The type of fixture, the reflective qualities of the walls and ceiling, the amount of natural light, and the distance from the fixture to the lighted surface will all affect the appropriate wattage for pleasing and effective illumination of your work surfaces.

Too much contrast between room and computer will cause eyestrain. To control ambient light, install dimmer switches and control light from windows with blinds or shades. To reduce eyestrain, maintain a low, even level of

The home office explosion in America is just beginning. Architects and designers, apartment dwellers and homeowners are struggling to find solutions for mixing work with leisure and for comfortably fitting family life into spaces that were originally designed without work in mind. This New York apartment, designed by Freya Block, is a careful orchestration of the mix, suggesting that creative enterprise has no bounds and that informal living can accommodate elements relating to one's work.

light in your home office, avoiding hot spots from lamps or other bright, single-source lights in the room while working at the computer. As you work, occasionally look out the window or through a doorway, focusing on a distant object for a few seconds.

Glare can also be a big problem. Position your monitor so that it is free of glare; if you have a brightness control button on your monitor, turn it down a bit. If daylight is significant, consider adjusting the angle of your computer screen to reduce reflection.

Remember that some lighting is easily moved as furniture and equipment configurations change, while other kinds of lighting—built into the ceiling, light decks, and affixed to walls—will be expensive to change. Also remember that you will have to change bulbs, so make sure that all fixtures are accessible.

Melinda Davidson equipped her home graphic design studio with overhead track lighting, which enabled her to slide the individual lights exactly where she needed illumination.

Sometimes she needed more light to work at her drafting table; other times client conferences required light at the other end of the studio. And there were days when she had twenty or thirty reference pictures spread around the floor and had to be able to look at one after another without eyestrain. Track lights to the rescue.

Windows

Natural light and fresh air are amenities of a home office often not available to those working in office buildings. The direction the windows face, the foliage on the site, the time of day, time of year, weather, and the part of the country where you live are all factors in determining the amount and kind of light that filters into your home office. In many North American climes, a southern exposure provides direct, harsh light, while a northern exposure is less direct, more diffuse.

Transoms, skylights, and clerestories can provide plenty of indirect light above sight lines and are a good choice if you are prone to gaze out windows and become distracted. The disadvantage is that most skylights and clerestories are forever opened to light and closed to fresh air (although attic skylights act more like windows and can be designed to open—some are prone to leak, however, so be careful what goes under them).

Windows at floor or desk height can be shaded or curtained, opened or shut. An operable window can warm up or cool off a home office that does not have its own thermal controls.

Elizabeth Haskell found that various styles of windows provided a means to let in air without catching breezes that would blow papers off her desk. Some windows opened in, some out, and some up. It was important to select a window style that would provide maximum protection if a sudden rainstorm whipped up while she was at the post office. Electronic equipment is sensitive to water, and a hard drive sitting on her desktop could become permanently defunct if drenched in a downpour. She decided that for her office's southern exposure, windows that opened in would afford the best weather protection while providing sufficient ventilation.

Except perhaps for an occasional slide show, opaque shades or curtains are usually unnecessary on office windows. Windows that receive harsh, direct light some of the time may need a more opaque covering than windows that receive only indirect sunlight.

Window treatment is ultimately a matter of taste and budget. Most people prefer some window covering for privacy, assuming that neighbors are close by. If the decor of your home office is closely integrated with the rest of your home, continuity of window treatments is an obvious solution. If your office is separate and "officelike," then a different style, such as miniblinds, may be more suitable.

The design of New York apartments has been a leading influence on home office solutions. For the creative professions, the expense of Manhattan real estate has dictated a single space for living and working for many independent New York workers, beginning with artists' lofts and writers' studios in the 19th century.

This close integration and free-form exchange between work and play, family, social, and working relationships within crowded, even cramped spaces has helped to introduce office and home furniture scaled to apartment living, furniture with multiple uses, furniture with hidden features (such as Murphy beds and convertible sofas), and furniture design that can conform to virtually any space. Freya Block's design for a New York apartment, *opposite* and *page 89*, simply permits living and working to overlap within small spaces, so that a client visit or a social call is accommodated by the same functional arrangement.

Acoustics

If you are alone in your office, the only real acoustical problem you'll have is keeping outside noise outside, whether it's coming from your neighbor's blaring stereo or a leaf blower. For a typical home office in the suburbs, the good news is that most houses are empty during the day, and most neighborhoods are relatively quiet when school is in session. The bad news is that every conceivable distracting noise from outside—from fire trucks, lawn services, motorcycles, boom boxes—will most likely find its way into your office. For new additions using conventional residential building methods, complete soundproofing is nearly impossible or prohibitively expensive.

Large offices use sound barrier screens to shield or muffle sounds between workstations. These sound-absorbent surfaces are not very attractive and are probably unnecessary for most two-person offices since interaction is often important. However, smaller panels are available that attach to walls and can be cut to size.

In general, hard surfaces reflect sound and soft surfaces, such as carpets and curtains, absorb it. Books and wood absorb sound better than glass and wallboard. Angling a ceiling may substantially increase sound absorption. Wood stud construction under gypsum wallboard absorbs sound better than metal studs. One layer of insulation under wallboard provides additional absorption; two layers, even more.

Flooring

Three important considerations in selecting flooring are wear, maintenance, and convenience. Given the small amount of traffic in most home offices, quality materials—vinyl or rubber tile, hardwood, or carpeting—should last a long time. Hardwood floors look great when they are kept clean and polished or finished with polyurethane. If you enjoy rolling around your office at high speed on the casters of your desk chair, a hard floor—

wood, rubber, or vinyl—may be the right choice. Stone, concrete, or ceramic tiles are cold, hard, and essentially inappropriate for home offices. There are hundreds of other tile and hardwood solutions, too, ranging from very cheap to impossibly expensive.

Carpeting has many distinct advantages over tile and hardwood floors. Noise-reduction leads to better efficiency and should be an important consideration. Carpeting also reduces dust and provides a soft, comfortable surface for your feet, particularly when performing chores that require standing, such as making photocopies. Carpeting also requires less maintenance than other finishes. It is easier to vacuum a carpet than to clean and wax a floor.

Elizabeth Haskell found that the casters on her desk chair were wearing down the pile in her carpeting. To counter this, she placed a clear plastic, carpet-protecting mat beneath the chair. Plastic mats are available for different situations: low-pile or deep-pile carpeting, hard floors, and one specifically for static control. Because he cruised all over his office in his chair and didn't want to be limited by a mat, **Jim Forrest** purchased a chair with casters specifically designed for carpeting.

By using a relatively flat, industrial-type carpet with a thin pad, normal chair or file cabinet movement across the carpet should not be a problem. Thick, well-padded carpet, like the kind you would use in a living room or bedroom, will absorb more sound and provide greater warmth but is not very practical. Wool carpeting wears best but is expensive and should be treated for stain resistance. Nylon or one of the other synthetic fibers is a better value for a home office but may require treatment to reduce static electricity buildup (either by using a static-reduction spray or having the carpeting treated by the carpet dealer upon purchase). Carpets of natural or synthetic fibers are available in a variety of weaves, styles, and colors. Flat, tightly woven carpeting, in a neutral or dark color, solid or with a subtle pattern, is the best choice for a professional office where comfort and efficiency are paramount.

Walls

The two most efficient things to have on the walls of your home office are storage systems and light-colored reflective expanses. Elaborate wall coverings like expensive textile wallpaper often hinder lighting solutions, although some are especially designed to deaden sound.

Consider the function of your walls before selecting a covering merely for its appearance. **Melinda Davidson**, who made several design decisions which later required costly changes, believes that one of her worst choices involved wall coverings. She first painted her walls a bright white, to promote a lighter, cheerier look in what she considered a rather dingy space. The white walls produced too much glare and, eventually, contributed to occasional migraine headaches. After a year she decided to repaint and chose the most common, practical, and least expensive solution: a creamy off-white acrylic paint over the original painted wallboard. She accented the off-white walls with dark blue trim around the windowsill and the door, selecting the same color for pulls on a closet and cabinet drawers.

As a general rule, keep your walls clean and simple, avoiding the lightest, brightest shades of white as well as avoiding dark colors, which deaden light.

Imaginative color and decorative wall schemes can be achieved with paint and some careful planning, such as in this home office of an art appraiser in a Victorian apartment in the Jordan Park district of San Francisco. The walls were decorated with elements designed by Maria and Daniel Levin of Interior Surface Arts.

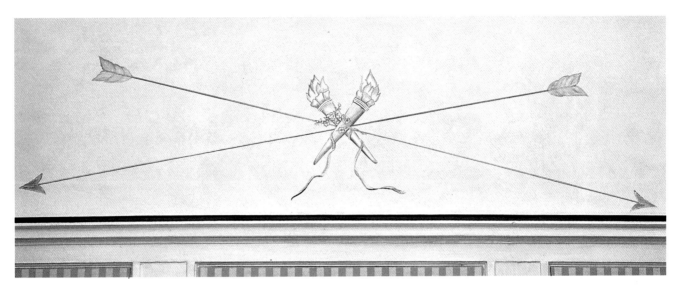

Heating, Ventilation, Air Quality, and Cooling (HVAC)

Heating, ventilation, air quality, and cooling (HVAC) require expert evaluation. If you are expanding existing space in your home and hope to avoid the expense of additional heating and cooling equipment, you may want to get advice from someone who is not in the business of selling you a new or expanded system. Your architect or builder will be helpful, but you may also need to engage a heating contractor or consultant to carefully evaluate present loads on your system. In some cases it may be less expensive to install a new, larger capacity furnace for the whole house than to add another unit for the addition. Or you may decide to switch from oil to natural gas or to add a heat pump to your existing system.

Other considerations relate to how your house is used while you're at work. If you are working full time during the day in your home office, does the rest of the house need to be heated or cooled at the same temperature? For large offices, HVAC is planned to optimize flexibility, control, and zoning. For a home office, this level of sophistication may by impractical or unnecessary. Like every other part of a home office construction project, consider your needs carefully and budget accordingly.

Keep in mind that computer equipment generates heat. If your home office is a small room with a number of electronic devices, keeping it cool may be a bigger issue than warming it up. Having a window that you can open when the office gets too warm (assuming it is cooler outside) will solve some of the problem; turning off your equipment when it is not in use will also help.

As you plan, consider the need or desirability for an electrostatic air cleaner (particularly if smokers will be using the office) and a humidifier. Air quality control is critical for those with allergies and other respiratory ailments. Air cleaners, humidifiers, dehumidifiers, and static eliminators employ differing technologies and run the gamut from rather simple and cheap to highly complex and expensive.

A bathroom may be the single most expensive item in a home office budget. Planning the location of your work space in relation to available plumbing or an existing bathroom, *above*, will save thousands of dollars.

Plumbing

Only major home office construction projects require new plumbing. For solo offices with only occasional visitors, installing a toilet and sink is probably an unnecessary expense. However, for offices with one or two employees in addition to yourself, suitable accommodation must be made. Keep in mind that even with a contractor on site, a half bath will add $2,000–5,000 to your project costs. If you must add plumbing to your project, consider adding a pocket kitchen as well, with a small sink, refrigerator, microwave, and coffeemaker; your employees and colleagues will appreciate it, and it will be useful for entertaining visitors.

When they exist, office restrooms are usually not designed as contemplative places. A small sink and toilet in a closet-sized space are all that is necessary. Remember, keeping you and your work separated from your home life is often an important objective for creating an efficient home office. Adequate plumbing is simply one way to meet that goal.

Electrical Requirements

In any home office situation, having sufficient power and grounded outlets are essential. Old houses may require some rewiring so that three-pronged plugs can be used. Voltage irregularities in household current and power outages plague many areas and may be one of the few problems that remain in equipping a high-tech home office. Some residential areas are prone to outages because electrical cables are on poles above ground (in most urban business areas, cables are buried below the streets) and can become victim to fallen tree limbs and other accidents caused by the weather and by traffic. Without emergency battery power, home office work tends to come to a halt when the power is out.

But power quality, including voltage fluctuations, power outages, and power surges, can be regulated by various devices. Whether you need any of them depends on how critical your work product is; they can be expensive to install. In many jurisdictions the power company will provide (for a fee) an uninterrupted power supply (UPS) device that automatically provides battery-generated power to a single computer system for about fifteen minutes, enough time to save your work. It also protects the computer from power spikes and surges, kicking in automatically for a few milliseconds as needed.

According to Nancy Moses of the electric utility PEPCO, "whole house surge protectors that are installed at an electric meter or a T pole-top have not yet proven themselves, and tend to be expensive." For most home offices, the only critical appliance worth protecting against brief outages is the computer. If three people are working in a home office, three UPS services may be required (at about $10–15 each per month).

This same service is also available for purchase, its cost based on the number of amps that your computer equipment, including hard drives, draws. A less costly alternative is a line conditioner, or surge suppressor, that provides some protection against power fluctuations but does not provide battery-generated power backup during a blackout.

What Is Power Quality?

Power quality is more noticeable today because so many household appliances work from solid-state electronics that are sensitive to voltage fluctuations. The blinking 12:00 on your VCR or coffeemaker may be caused by fluctuations in the power coming into your house. Raw, high-voltage power is stepped down by transformers at substations through a system, finally coming down your street at 13,000 volts and then into your house at 112 or 220 volts. If you are at the end of a feeder line, the voltage may be slightly less consistent on some energy intensive days, as power users up the line draw more than their share to run their air conditioners full blast.

While there is really nothing practical that you can do about it except install a UPS or line conditioning system, make sure that you do not make the mistake **Greg Simpson** made. When he tried to run his computer, a voltage sensitive machine, on the same circuit as his refrigerator, it resulted in erratic spikes in power that affected the operations of his plugged-in laptop computer.

Surprisingly, many of the powerful electronic devices in today's high-tech offices consume relatively small amounts of energy. A Macintosh at idle burns energy at about the rate of a 30-watt light bulb. Machines requiring heat or high-intensity light, such as copiers and fax printers, require more power. Power consumption of a fax machine at standby is less than 10 watts; while sending or receiving, about 175 watts; a typical medium-sized copier consumes 1,500 watts during operations. For those devices requiring large amounts of power, a dedicated line may be necessary, depending on the capacity of the circuits in your office. Obviously, an electrician, working with your designer or contractor, will plan this out for you once you know your power consumption requirements.

The cost of power consumption can vary greatly if your area or neighborhood has time-of-use rates (also called peak-load pricing). Since most residences consume less power during the early morning hours and late at night, your power rates can be substantially reduced if your power company provides this service (which includes installation of a device that measures your power consumption by time of day) and if you work during off-peak hours.

Home office settings such as these rooms, designed for a client by **Bill Stubbs**, suggest that some home workers simply follow the sun, working in various places around the house, on the deck, or by the pool with only a laptop computer and a cordless telephone.

With the miniaturization of equipment and the increasingly clever ways that furniture makers disguise equipment and file storage, some home offices do not even look like offices at all.

Safety and Security Considerations

Home security and fire protection relate only to efficient office design if someone breaks into your office or it burns down. If either occurs, your contingency planning may be the only buffer between rapid recovery and complete annihilation of your home-based business. There are several concerns relating to fire protection and security.

Installing a battery-powered smoke detector, particularly in an area of the office where there is a heat-producing device (such as a space heater, coffeemaker, or high-intensity lamp) is cheap and easy. If you are wiring for new construction, consider installing an electric smoke detector with a battery backup. Having a small fire extinguisher on hand is also wise.

Fire prevention and detection is another matter. The design of a fire detection system extends from the placement of a fire extinguisher and smoke detector to the selection of fire retardant materials and a floor plan that permits easy and rapid evacuation.

Because of several break-ins in her neighborhood, **Melinda Davidson** constantly worried about the security of her home office when she was away. Admitting that she's "simply paranoid," Melinda spoke with consultants and examined several home security systems. Her first choice was one that combined burglar alarms—silent alarms, light and motion detectors, sound alarms—with whole house power interruption security (see page 93), remote access, and timers that control every electrical device in her house, turning lights, television sets, the coffeemaker, and other appliances on and off at predetermined yet varied times. When the bids came in, she was shocked to discover that a whole house system cost more than $10,000. She settled on a better lock for the back door and an ingenious device, which cost only $90, that turned lights on and off at regular intervals when she and her husband were away.

Home Security Consider the following to help ensure better home security:

- Don't leave your house exposed. Erect a fence or plant shrubs and hedges around your house.

- Get a dog.

- Lock all doors and windows. Use dead-bolt locks for your doors.

- Keep your house well lit.

- Hire a private patrol service.

- Create the appearance of being at home even when you are not.

- Install a security system.

- Use a reliable housesitter when you go out of town.

- Have your house inspected by a security specialist (some police departments offer this service).

- Store important papers and other valuables in a home safe or in a safety deposit box at your bank.

Offices located in homes secluded from other houses or the street are particularly vulnerable to intruders when left unattended and unsecured.

Security systems, while expensive, offer protection, as does a well-lit driveway and walk and some evidence of habitation inside, such as lights turning off and on from timers or a radio or television set left on.

Doors and windows that are accessible to visitors are also accessible to others. Leave them locked, and if facing the street, covered with shades or curtains.

Elizabeth Haskell considers her standing in her neighborhood as important to her security as locks, alarms, and dogs. Caring and watchful neighbors are, to her, perhaps the best defense against burglary. Obviously, when other people with home offices are out and about the neighborhood during the day it certainly helps. The presence of cyclists, joggers, strollers, and people with flex-time work schedules also helps. But in general Elizabeth feels that by having good locks and thoughtful neighbors, your chances of having a burglar-free house are much better than if you invest in a lot of fancy equipment and remain a stranger on your street.

Although a good lock and a home security system are both worthy of consideration, you must also be sensitive to the placement of your home office relative to the street or alley. If the interior of a home office with expensive electronic equipment can be viewed from the outside, it may become an inviting target for a break-in.

Security within your home requires similar caution. For workers who deal with sensitive materials, such as lawyers and accountants, an office with a lockable door or cabinet may be necessary to maintain accountability of documents. Computer security may also be necessary to ensure peace of mind or simply to keep your children off your hard drive. Computer security involves both hardware—a lock that prevents a computer from being carried away—and software, usually in the form of a password to either start the computer, activate a particular program, or open a file. Differing needs can be accommodated by a range of software products available for office security.

CHAPTER 3
SELECTING FURNITURE

The world's storage rooms and used furniture outlets seem to be filling up with dented and used gray, green, and beige metal desks and filing cabinets as offices modernize and downsize and as computer filing systems proliferate.

In general, home office decor and furnishings fall into three categories:

- •eclectic, easy, and inexpensive
- •home sweet home
- •streamlined efficiency

The first approach is the most common. Spare parts assembled from your commercial office, your child's room, a tag sale, an office furniture closeout sale, or a piece or two from a discount warehouse provide a comfortable arrangement. Many technologically sophisticated home workers can't imagine spending hard-earned money on matching furniture when the same funds could buy a faster computer, more memory, or a bigger monitor.

The second approach to a home office is more subtle, strategic, and sophisticated: a home office decorated to look like a living room, study, bedroom, den, pub, or Edwardian library. Both men and women often think of their home office as simply an extension of the rest of their house. They may even use the space as an office during the day and a living area at night, although most people want to separate work and nonwork areas in their daily lives. These homelike offices are masters of disguise: a copier is stowed in a closet or armoire, a CPU under an antique rolltop desk.

The third model for home offices follows more traditional office criteria established for large companies over the past half century by such famous designers as Marcel Breuer, Serge Chermayeff, Charles Eames, and Florence Knoll. An alternate approach is a modular office system, with small, discretionary or interchangeable pieces placed together in various configurations. A principal innovator in modular home office systems has been Marshall Erdman's Techline system.

Today many office furniture manufacturers are rapidly scaling down their products and prices to fit the home office market, with design leaders such as Herman Miller and Steelcase at the forefront of this movement.

The arm on the Ergon 2® chair, designed by Bill Stumpf for Herman Miller, is adjustable.

Desks and Surfaces

Your home office will probably need extensive desktop and countertop space. While you will need space for a lot of equipment—hard drives, CD-ROM player, speakers, scanner, printer, fax machine, answering machine, two or three telephones, countertop copier, tape dispenser, lamps, pencil holder, stapler, paper clip dispenser, paperweights, and a calculator—it is also convenient to have space on which to write a letter in longhand, spread out receipts while working on taxes or expense reports, or map strategies for new projects. Unfortunately, surface space, like the space on your hard drive, often fills up quickly and may never be clean again.

A person working on a computer has different desk needs from one who works with pen and pad. Obviously, computer equipment requires much more surface space. Less obvious is the need for more knee room. The dynamics of working at a computer require the ability to move around a bit, swiveling in your chair, shifting slightly left and right as you move a mouse across a mouse pad, place a disk into a disk drive, load paper in a printer, and perform other routine tasks.

While a majority of home workers will probably purchase a conventional desk, an increasing number will require more space. Two solutions are

The "paperless office" was promoted a decade ago as the wave of the future, the result of magnetic storage for data and documents, and the widespread use of electronic mail and other telecommunications applications. In fact, more hard copy documents and mail land on office desks today than ever before, proving that information used in business decision-making is rapidly expanding in every possible direction, regardless of the media.

Desktops are the repository for much of this hard copy, which remains in neat stacks or cascades across every available surface until it is thrown away, passed along, or filed. It seems that no matter how much space is allotted, there is never enough.

This office configuration, *below*, includes a pie-shaped "filler" to provide continuity to the desk surfaces arranged at right angles.

purchasing a workstation or building a countertop. Workstations are usually L-shaped, fitting into the corner of a room. They provide about twice the work space of a traditional desk, and they offer a variety of cubbyholes, drawers, cabinets, and cabling raceways specifically designed to place, store, and hide equipment and wires.

Desktop and workstation levels come in two standard heights: the work surface is usually 28 or 29 inches from the floor; the surface on which a keyboard sits is typically 24.5 to 28 inches from the floor. If you can only install a single height for a desktop or cannot install a keyboard tray under your desk, the height of your desktop should be 28 inches. Adjusting your chair and using a footrest can compensate for the differences between the ideal height for keyboard operations and other tasks at the desktop.

The depth of your desktop may vary considerably. A minimum depth is 21 inches, which is sufficient to fit a microcomputer (with a monitor on top), assuming that a keyboard tray will be mounted underneath. More typical depths range from 25 to 30 inches. Base cabinets and files for modular systems are typically available in 20- and 24-inch depths to be placed below 21- and 25-inch-deep tops. Architects using a computer-aided design, or CAD, workstation, as well as some artists and designers working

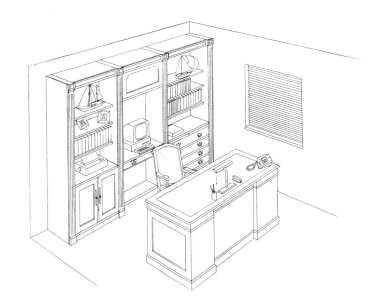

with very large monitors, may require considerably more depth, perhaps 40 inches or more. Other specialized workstations, such as a sample area for an interior designer, are configured for standing or sitting, with a counter height from 39 to 43 inches and a seat height of 27 to 30 inches from the floor.

Counter configurations that place the task area in a corner create greater depth for the immediate work area, but less depth extending right and left from the corner. By truncating the corner and adding a suspended, adjustable keyboard beneath the counter, you can add a

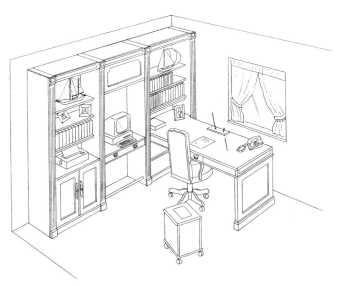

The watchword for desking these days is flexibility, with furniture designers inventing multiple configurations for varying spaces, equipment needs, and worker preferences. These two sketches for planning desk and work space are from Sligh Furniture Company. The combination of closed and open shelving, accommodation for wiring, allowance for the depth of a large monitor, a keyboard tray, and other features that facilitate comfort and accessibility, have begun to revolutionize office furniture design.

High-concept contract furniture for small and home offices, such as the **TAO** collection from Davis Furniture Industries, is being joined in the marketplace by new offerings that can be found in retail outlets such as Crate and Barrel Furniture or office supply mega-stores such as Staples. The **TAO** collection is a modular series of desks, *above*, workstations and credenzas, *opposite*, file storage, *left*, and pedestals and conference tables that can be combined in a variety of configurations.

Two basic approaches to desks are represented here by a system of continuous laminated countertops in the Techline system, *opposite,* **and a more traditional approach incorporating an oak desk,** *above.* **The traditional desk is less flexible but more appropriate when blending with other residential furniture.**

great deal of usable surface space without significantly enlarging the area of the whole counter system.

Workstations and desks are usually constructed of a composite material covered with a veneer, although some fine furniture companies now manufacture solid wood units for home office use. The veneers available for home office workstations, desks, and counters can be coordinated with finishes on other home furniture, such as oak, cherry, or rosewood, with kitchen counter surfaces, or with materials typical of office surfaces. These tough, stain- and scuff-resisting synthetic materials are available in light gray, beige, or off-white to match computer equipment and walls.

A curvilinear Steelcase desk was used by Mary Ann McEwan for her design of a home office and reception area at a 1992 designer showcase house in Woodside, California.

As home offices become a standard feature in American homes, furniture manufacturers have become increasingly inventive in the design of desks that blend into their surroundings. This maple and white home office is by Techline.

Chairs

Only recently have office furniture companies moved away from occupational and gender distinctions in the classification of seating. Because executives and secretaries require essentially the same ergonomic features in a "task" chair, the determining factor in selecting a chair has more to do with body size than with gender, income, or status. Anyone who works at a computer for most of the day should look for a chair with separate adjustments for lumbar and lower back support, arm width and height, seat back angle, and seat height. Typically, these chairs have a seat adjustment from 17 to 22 inches.

The ultimate in office seating and seating accessories for the home office includes a comfortable and ergonomically designed desk chair. Bulldog Task Armchair from **The Knoll Group**, *lower right*; a footrest, *below*; a side chair for visitors, *above*; and lounge chairs and ottomans for reading, napping, or conversing, *opposite*.

© NORTH COAST MEDICAL, INC.

Ergonomic office chairs offer adjustable arms and backs, as well as height, tension, and angle control to align and support all body types correctly. Until recently, desk chairs were sized and styled in "secretary," "manager," and "executive" sizes. As all office work has now evolved toward the computer, desk chairs have been redesigned to be more functional and less related to employment status. For example, the Patriot Executive chair, *opposite*, is a high-back chair with a seat height that adjusts from 17 to 22 inches. The Patriot Office Chair, *left*, has the same adjustments as the Executive Chair, but in a mid-back style.

© NORTH COAST MEDICAL, INC.

A footrest provides additional back support, particularly for workers of short stature who need to "raise the floor" as part of their seating adjustment. This model has multiple positions and is easily adjusted by the slightest pressure from the feet. It even moves with your feet when you stretch your legs.

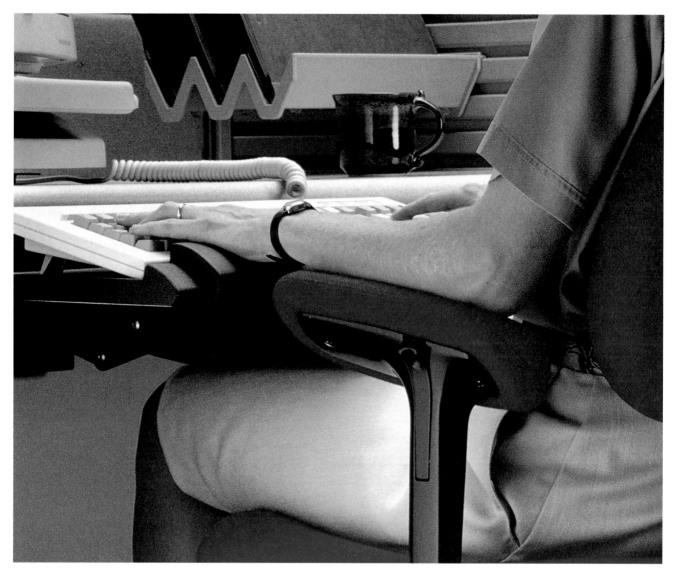

The best-quality task chairs are available with adjustable armrests that help to lessen back, shoulder, and neck strain.

The wrist rest, *above*, is most effective as a place to rest during work pauses rather than as you work. It is also not always comfortable or practical to maintain arm and elbow support while typing, although chairs with adjustable arm rests, such as this Ergon 2® from Herman Miller, provide this feature.

Designers Ross Lovegrove and Stephen Peart developed these biomorphic shapes for Knoll by determining the frequency of various motions in using computers. The wrist pads in front help keep the wrists in a neutral position when at rest, lessening strain; a matching mouse pad is at right.

Saving Your Wrists

Workers who spend a majority of their day on a keyboard often suffer from repetitive stress injury (RSI), also called carpal-tunnel syndrome. RSI can be experienced as a slight numbness or an acute pain, a temporary problem or a permanent injury. Andy Ihnatko, a columnist for *MacUser* magazine, suggests that at the first sign of trouble, you consult your physician, who will probably suggest some behavior modification and perhaps a brace, which should be used correctly. He suggests that "wrist rests" be used during pauses rather than as a place to put your wrists while typing, which only makes matters worse.

When typing, it is best to keep your wrists in a neutral position, rather than extended or flexed, according to Sharon McKenzie, a consulting occupational therapist for an office safety products company. She recommends that people with potential problems have a job task analysis performed by an occupational or physical therapist or a health and safety engineer (if you are a telecommuter working for a big company). Such a specialist can evaluate the position of your wrists, arms, back, and neck as you perform usual tasks, and then provide recommendations for support devices, chair and screen positions, counter and keyboard height, and other adjustments to your workstation.

File Storage and Shelving

A vexing problem for home office workers is the rapid accumulation, and subsequent need for storage, of paper. Books, laser outtakes, file copies, mail, documentation, sales promotion literature, proceedings, printouts, magazines, faxes, receipts, and newspapers all flood across desks and counters, stacked in cartons, on shelves, or on the floor. According to Emily Gordon, owner of a Birmingham, Alabama, store, Let's Get Organized, "the mail and other important papers are the key category for consumer organization....We are constantly getting requests from customers for something in which to file mail."

At one time the promise of the electronic office was that it would become a paperless office, yet it appears that in reality the reverse is true: the greater the advances in office electronics, the greater the amount of paper generated. Whether you try to conserve paper or are ruthless in discarding unnecessary surplus, keeping the volume of paper down to a manageable level is a constant problem. Given the wasted paper generated by a laser printer in most home offices, consider reusing the opposite side for drafts and other internal purposes. Some people also shred paper for use as packing material, while others save scrap and discarded paper for recycling. Beyond the issues of reuse and disposal of paper, a variety of other storage decisions confronts every home office.

Your storage needs are not static. It is important to develop a strategy for managing paper, or you will forever be searching your house for a lost file or storage box. While it may seem impractical to set aside accessible storage space either in your home office itself or a designated area in your house, in the long run you will save time, money, and aggravation. Don't scatter boxes of papers all over the house. Keeping home and office separate—including storage—can become critical to an efficient organization system.

Within Reach? As you design your space, think carefully about storage:

- What do you need within arm's reach of your desk?
- Would a rolling file be useful next to your desk?
- What do you need in a handy location within your home office?
- What can be relegated to a garage, attic, or other location on-site?
- Do you need off-site storage at a rented facility?

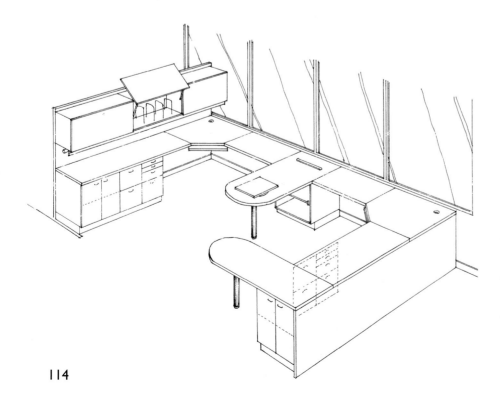

A busy offices requires various kinds of storage, from file cabinets, to open shelving, to drawers, to storage boxes, to cubby holes, to closets. File storage in a Techline configuration, *left*, can include both base cabinets below and wall-hung cabinets above. Storage boxes, *right*, help to keep magazines organized.

Home Office Strategy: File Storage

After seventeen years in a downtown Washington office I had accumulated a mountain of archives and other materials. Reducing this to something manageable took weeks. I had used an off-site storage facility, a locker where I stacked about 100 cardboard Banker's Boxes filled with printing samples of my graphic design and publishing work and business records for the IRS. Before moving, I reduced the number of boxes to about twenty and transferred them to my attic, where I was able to reduce the number further as tax records from previous years were discarded.

Moving these ugly but extremely useful cardboard boxes around in my attic over the years convinced me that they were an ideal storage container, and I incorporated them into a storage system when designing my home office. A space 24 inches deep, 84 inches high, and 120 inches long was configured as a closet with floor to ceiling open shelving to accommodate as many as eighty Banker's Boxes. At about $3.00 apiece, these boxes provided more than 100 linear feet of file storage for a total of $240. The boxes hold only sixteen inches of files, so the weight is never more than about twenty-five pounds.

I now maintain a rotation system, since each project that I complete requires between two and five of these boxes, which must each be retained for several years. As I work on current projects, I maintain research and other files in filing cabinets that are part of my office system. I also keep my permanent files—insurance, banking, incorporation, and other business documents—handy. When I no longer require daily use of project files, I transfer them to the closet, where they remain for up to a year. Periodically, I move these boxes from the closet to the attic. The boxes in the attic contain older files; those that are no longer needed are discarded and the boxes reused. This storage system can expand considerably, since I use only about half the closet space—which is only a few feet from my desk—for file storage.

As your home-based business grows, so will your mail, with piles arranged on every available surface if you do not manage and organize the flow as it comes in the door. Many residential communities recycle newspapers and magazines, but few recycle non-newsprint printed paper. The storage device for mail that is most used in my home office is round and is filled nearly to the brim everyday—the wastebasket.

Some people like a cluttered, "lived-in" look, while others want their office to be neat and tidy, with a place for everything. Either way, a system of appropriately defined storage is necessary for an efficient office: Close at hand, you'll need stamps, pencils, a box of tissues, a mouse pad. At the opposite extreme, you'll need some place for "dead" storage, for old tax records and project files.

At the middle landscape of your office, storage systems for books, magazines, files, software, office supplies, tools, and stationery each require a somewhat different solution, requiring advance planning and periodic reorganization and cleanup.

This home office, designed by Oakland, California, designer Shelli Oreck, also functions as a guest room, with a bed on the wall adjacent to the bookshelf.

Home Office Strategy: Bookshelves

One of the advantages of having my own office space is that reference materials and a whole library of books are constant companions in my work. Books are my trade; as a writer-designer and book producer, I use them constantly.

Over the years I had accumulated a library of more than 4,000 volumes, about half paperbacks and half hardcover. When I worked downtown, my books were divided between home and office—and invariably the book I needed was at the other place. Because I had a weekend retreat as well as a storage facility, I found over time that my books were in fact scattered over four locations, with still more at my parents' house in Alabama.

As I began to plan my home office, one important part of my mission was to consolidate my library. I had always thought it would be impossible to discard books,

but a perusal of my collection revealed that I could easily reduce the number of truly useful titles by more than 50 percent, distributing the excess to a used bookstore, my local library, and family members.

I stored what remained of my library in moving boxes until my office was constructed. Freestanding shelving that I'd had built some years before was incorporated into my home office plan, with some molding strips added and a few other minor adjustments made by a carpenter as he installed the shelving.

I still must weed out obsolete titles as my library grows and changes. Many books that I never use remain on the shelves as fond reminders of earlier interests, references to research projects long past that provided some great insight or simply gave me pleasure.

Shelving Guidelines

Since there is never enough shelf space in an office, plan to devote as much wall space as possible to as much shelving as is practical. In general, for book and magazine shelving, keep these points in mind:

- Heavy metal prefabricated industrial shelving is sturdy and practical but looks terrible. Place this in a storage room or have cabinets built to house it.
- Epoxy-coated wire closet shelving, available at hardware stores and home improvement centers, is designed to hold clothing and sometimes food items for the kitchen, but usually not books, which are too heavy. These are intended for mounting into drywall and may not be sturdy enough for office use.
- Small, inexpensive bookcases, purchased unassembled, are useful. Floor-to-ceiling versions of these bookcases may not be sufficiently sturdy to hold books. If you purchase a large bookcase, each shelf should only be about thirty inches wide. Wider shelves tend to bow with the weight of books.
- If you are constructing or contracting to construct built-in bookshelves, a fascia, or strip of wood affixed to the facing of the shelf, will significantly increase its rigidity.
- Measure your books by height to get an idea of the ratio of tall shelves for large books to smaller shelves for paperbacks.

For other shelving needs, it is important to consider what materials and supplies should remain behind closed doors and what should be out in the open. Office supplies, reams of paper, extra computer cables, and tools should be tucked away, while other items should be placed on open shelves for greater accessibility.

The home office of interior designer Gail Whiting in Bridgewater, New Jersey, *opposite*, was designed with an entire wall of bookshelves.

Levenger Project Box, *right*. Ten years ago the paperless office was on its way as forecasters predicted that electronic communications would begin to eliminate paper and printing. In fact the opposite happened. As faxes, laser printers, and copiers proliferated, the speed of communications increased, requiring more, not less paper. What to keep and what to discard, what should be on your desk, in a file drawer, or in a storage box becomes a nagging question for any knowledge worker.

Office organization and storage has become a big industry, with consultants, manufacturers, and retailers all developing an endless supply of storage solutions and organizational tools that are attractive, functional, and inexpensive.

A book box system, *above*, and a desk organizer, *left*, shelving for a very narrow space, *opposite top*, and a traditional desk designed for computer operations, *opposite below*, are all designed to blend into residential settings, yet serve in office environments.

Modularity, that is, the ability to mix and match different pieces in a grouping, has become the challenge for virtually all new home office furniture systems. The cherry computer desk, *below*, from Levenger, is actually a computer desk with a pull-out keyboard tray, a storage cabinet on the left, and a three-drawer file cabinet on the right.

For offices that are part of living areas, the trick is either to hide the true purpose of a piece of furniture or make it sufficiently elegant and appropriate to the room's decor so that its business function is muted.

Designers, cabinetmakers, and furniture manufacturers are constantly challenged by the ever-changing sizes, shapes, and endless configurations of computers, printers, and monitors, attempting to create flexible systems that will accommodate present and future technologies.

This home office, *opposite* and *above*, was designed by Richard and Shelley Hall of Richard L. Hall Enterprises, Orange, California. The open-legged writing table was designed by Bevan Funnell.

Across from the desk, *opposite*, is a high-low remote-controlled mahogany computer cabinet from Bevan Funnell, *left top* and *bottom*. Beyond is a display cabinet, *above*.

CHAPTER 4
SELECTING OFFICE EQUIPMENT

You have now planned, designed, and built your new home office. You've added attractive and functional desks, chairs, and counters, along with enough shelving and storage space to last a while. Now all you need is the equipment to get your business up and running, and chances are that most of your equipment will be electronic.

Every electronic device has either circuitry or some other set of instructions that tell it what to do. For a calculator or digital watch, all of these instructions exist on a microchip. For a computer, these instructions exist on microchips of varying sizes (hardware) and as written code (software) that combines with the work of microchips to tell the computer what to do. When you set the time on your watch or press keys on a calculator, you are giving instructions. On a computer, you provide input through a keyboard, mouse, stylus, or perhaps a scanner to provide instructions.

Telephones, answering machines, fax machines, printers, copiers, and other electronic wizardry in your home office are guided and controlled by some combination of you, the software, and the hardware. Each of these machines communicates to you through a *user interface*. For a watch, the user interface is either hands pointing to numbers or a digital readout. On your fax machine, it is probably a small LED window providing instructions and other messages.

User interfaces can be clear and straightforward or highly cryptic, and their usefulness depends on the manufacturer's ability to present an understandable, or at least easy-to-figure-out, method of communication between you and the machine. Some electronic devices maintain little or no direct communication with you, but are slaves to another gadget and are dependent on their user interface. For example, the external hard drive for your computer has only an on-off switch with an indicator light to interface with you directly, but it makes enormous amounts of information available to you through its operating system and various programs.

Understanding the user interface of the equipment you are purchasing is the first criterion in its selection. You also will want to evaluate its features, supply requirements, maintenance cycle, and general usefulness against its cost, the amount of time it will take for you to learn to use and maintain it, and the amount of space it will occupy. These criteria apply to your choice of computers and peripherals, copiers and fax machines, and telecommunication equipment and services.

Perhaps the greatest challenge for home office workers is keeping abreast of rapidly changing technology. Computers, telecommunications, and imaging devices become faster, better, and less expensive with each turn of the calendar. Techline components, *opposite*, easily incorporate new technologies.

Computer Hardware and Peripherals

At many big corporations, mainframe and minicomputers are being replaced by workstations and microcomputers. Virtually all computerized home offices contain microcomputers.

Which microcomputing system to use? This decision has been reduced in recent years to a choice between two major hardware systems, based on either Intel or Motorola chips. Intel chips (including a few clones) are used in IBM-compatible computers, called personal computers or PCs, and Motorola chips in Apple Macintosh computers, called Macs. These hardware standards, also called "platforms," will eventually change through a major joint venture between IBM and Apple, but the two differing computer cultures will probably remain as such for some time.

Operating systems—which include the set of instructions that provides the user interface for a computer—have been reduced to three principal systems: PCs use either Microsoft Corporation's DOS or Windows, and Macs use Apple's System 7.

The Macintosh is different from DOS (an acronym for Disk Operating System) and Windows in that its user interface is consistently applied to virtually all Macintosh programs, so that all Macintosh software can be operated using essentially the same sequence of steps. Windows superficially mimics the Macintosh user interface, but its software tends to be inconsistent in how it interfaces with your hard drive and how its introductory or desktop screen looks. This is an important difference between the two systems. Computers running DOS tend to be less expensive, more readily available in the used-computer market, and easier and less expensive to repair; DOS is the operating system employed by nearly a hundred million computers.

Computer-literate office workers fall into two categories: those who consider computer equipment as simply a time-saving tool and those who become fascinated with the technology. For the second group, equipment proliferates, particularly in those offices where increased productivity translates directly to increased income.

For Turnstone, a Steelcase company, a priority is the small business market, for businesses located either in office buildings or at home. This small office/home office configuration, *opposite*, can accommodate additional equipment as business increases.

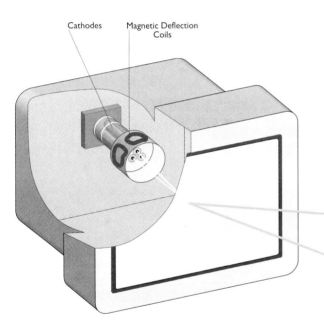

Cathodes   Magnetic Deflection Coils

A color monitor for a computer uses three cathodes (negatively charged electron emitters) that read red, green, and blue information and convert it to electron beams. Magnetic deflection coils bend the electron beams horizontally or vertically, aiming them at pixels on the screen. Each pixel contains three phosphors—one for red, one for blue, one for green. Phosphors are activated when hit by the electron beams, glowing red, green, or blue to simulate blended color.

While DOS uses a character-based interface, both Macintosh System 7 and Windows operating systems employ a *graphical* user interface, that is, one based on icons and various typographic and pictographic representations to help guide operations. The Macintosh System 7 interface combines a "menu" of basic operations at the top of the screen (such as "file" and "edit") with a "desktop" that holds various file "folders." You can select an operation, or open a folder, simply by positioning the pointer on it with your mouse.

Many computers marketed for home office use are packaged with an operating system and some software—word processing, spreadsheet, and graphics programs, for instance—already installed. Increasingly, word processing and spreadsheet files saved in Windows can be read by a Macintosh, or sometimes vice versa.

Macs cost more than PCs but are easier to set up and use and have features particularly suitable for graphics and presentations. Mac is the computer of choice for entrepreneurs and other independent home office workers. Telecommuters and part-time workers who work for large companies are more likely to select a PC, although personal preferences and former workplace biases play an important role in platform selection.

A basic computer system includes a central processing unit (CPU), keyboard, monitor, and a printer. The CPU, which contains the microprocessor chips and the hard drive, can sit on a desk, counter, or floor. If placed on your desk, it typically serves as a base or stand for the monitor. The printer, which connects to the computer by a cable, should be placed on a nearby work surface. You will also need room for the computer's keyboard, mouse, and mouse pad.

There are many other computer-related devices, called peripherals, that you may wish to leave room for as you plan your home office. These include a second hard drive (for additional data storage, since many software programs consume massive amounts of memory), a CD-ROM player, modem, scanner, or graphics tablet.

Wiring becomes a challenge when you are trying to install your computer equipment neatly; the growing number of peripherals creates a nest of jumbled cables. It is difficult to streamline and bundle these cables because they begin and end in different places: the mouse typically plugs into the keyboard, the keyboard into the CPU, and the CPU into a wall outlet, power strip, or surge protector. A number of products are available to help organize this mess, including cable "raceways," holders, covers, ducts, and fasteners. Some desks provide built-in cable management schemes, such as a hollow leg or a trough at the back of the desktop.

Among the infinite variety of computer accessories intended
to ease the aches and pains of keyboard work are a copy
holder that supports multiple documents and manuals,
above, and an adjustable monitor arm, *opposite*.

Recapturing desk space by mounting your monitor to a desktop or adjacent wall requires a sturdy and flexible spring-balanced arm, such as this one from **North Coast Medical.**

Selecting a Computer: Mac versus PC

Melinda Davidson ignored PCs entirely and went straight for a Macintosh for her graphic design studio, while **Greg Simpson** did not even look at Macs when he shopped for a laptop to use on the road and at home. For **Elizabeth Haskell** and **Jim Forrest**, the choice was not so clear. Haskell selected a Mac, Forrest a PC.

If any of them attempted to make an objective decision—which is better for me: Mac or PC, Windows or DOS?—based on discussions with computer sales personnel or neighborly advice from a computer expert, they no doubt would have been totally confused. Even the most thorough research will result in conflicting information. Perhaps to further confuse the matter, Apple has introduced Power Macintosh computers that are compatible with PC programs, while special "bridge" software allows PCs to run the Macintosh operating system.

You should base your computer selection on some combination of your computer training or lack thereof; the applications (i.e., software) that you will run; your interest or ability in tinkering with electronic devices; your budget; the system your coworkers, clients, or colleagues use; your fascination, or lack thereof, with new technology; and the presence of or accessibility to a mentor or consultant to help you through early learning stages.

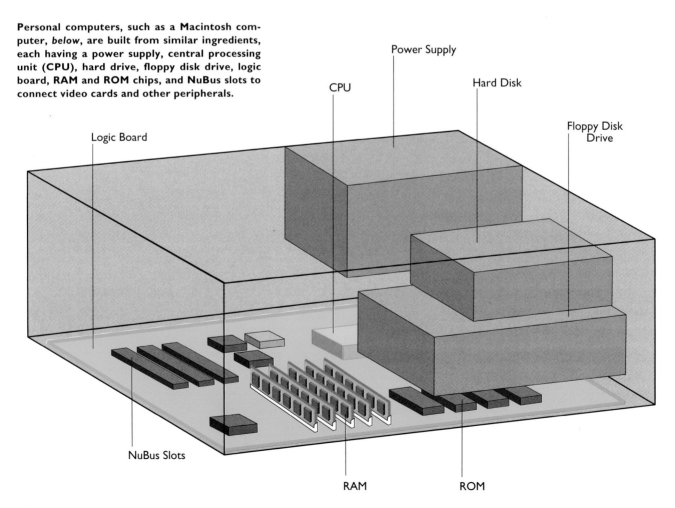

Personal computers, such as a Macintosh computer, *below*, **are built from similar ingredients, each having a power supply, central processing unit (CPU), hard drive, floppy disk drive, logic board, RAM and ROM chips, and NuBus slots to connect video cards and other peripherals.**

Power Supply

CPU

Hard Disk

Floppy Disk Drive

Logic Board

NuBus Slots

RAM

ROM

Any recommendation must be carefully evaluated, since not all home offices are the same and not all home office workers have the same requirements. The following checklist compares Macs and PCs; it may help you narrow the fundamental choice between the two basic platforms (• indicates preference).

Features/Functions

	Mac	PC
APPLICATIONS:		
Word processing	•	•
Spreadsheet	•	•
Graphics	•	
Personal finance	•	•
Database	•	•
Information manager	•	•
Electronic mail	•	•
EASE OF SET-UP:		
Network	•	
Fonts	•	
Peripherals	•	
FUNCTIONALITY:		
Multimedia	•	
Laptop	•	•
Speed	•	•
Productivity	•	
SUPPORT SERVICES:		
Repair		•
Documentation	•	•
Graphics output services	•	
Accessories	•	•
Media	•	•
Memory	•	•

When **Elizabeth Haskell** went shopping for a new computer system, she was most concerned about whether she could manage a two- or three-computer office without relying on an expensive consultant. Although she had used an IBM at her downtown office, she always relied on a systems administrator to install software and troubleshoot problems. On her own, she suspected that a PC-based system would be more than she could handle.

This issue—providing additional workstations for consulting accountants and an employee—was decisive for Elizabeth. If your home office program includes more than one computer, you will find it considerably more convenient to network the computers so that files produced on one can be accessed by others. This is a fairly simple process for Macintoshes, but a PC system would require professional help. For Haskell, the "plug-and-play" ease of the Mac was critically important.

Her software needs were simple. She required a good spreadsheet program and discovered that Microsoft Excel, the program she had always used, was available for the Mac. She also needed programs for word processing and for managing name and address files of her clients and vendors.

Haskell found that basic software for the Macintosh and for Windows had similar features, and that many of the most popular programs were available in either format. For word processing, spreadsheet, personal finance, database, information management, and electronic mail, the overall performance and features of these applications are comparable and, in some cases, the same. Microsoft Word, for example, is available for either system. A document she had produced in Microsoft Word on her IBM downtown could be read by a late-model Macintosh at home.

The only software category in which there is a substantial difference in performance and features is graphics, where the Macintosh maintains significant advantages over Windows. This advantage is what tipped the scales for **Melinda Davidson.** She knew that programs such as Aldus PageMaker and QuarkXPress, programs used by graphic designers, were available for either Macintosh- or Windows-based systems. In fact, at her former job, she used PageMaker on a powerful IBM computer running Windows, even though many of her designer friends scoffed that PCs were awkward and had limited usefulness for graphics applications.

At her job, Melinda relied on others for help with setup and fonts. On her own, she discovered that solving the problems with using Windows for graphics were beyond her interest or skill, relating to difficulties in setting-up peripherals (such as additional storage devices, a scanner,

or a graphics tablet). Using a variety of typographic fonts has always been a challenge for Windows-based systems, requiring a considerable number of counterintuitive and confusing steps to change, load, and apply multiple custom fonts for use in a document.

Jim Forrest was always intrigued by Macintosh technology but wound up with a powerful Compaq computer using a new Pentium chip. Talking with a computer professional from his Manhattan office, Jim learned that his company's proprietary online-searching software—which he used all day to make custom reports for clients—was only available for IBM-compatible PCs, not for the Mac. Jim and the computer wizard designed a home office system that was a virtual clone of the one in his downtown office, including the software. High-speed telecommunications was the critical capability, requiring special cabling and high-priced data services.

While distinctions between operating systems are not so important in laptop models per se, there is an apparent productivity gain by Macintosh users, for both laptop and desktop models. A 1994 study conducted by the highly respected Arthur D. Little, Inc., of Cambridge, Massachusetts, concluded that Macintosh users finished a variety of business tasks 44 percent faster than Windows users and were 50 percent more likely to finish their tasks correctly. The study measured the work habits of 100 business users performing 24 business tasks, such as editing documents, managing files, and printing.

Memory

Random Access Memory (RAM), Read-only Memory (ROM), and Parameter RAM (PRAM) are the brains of a computer. ROM consists of coded instructions on a silicon chip that help the computer perform basic housekeeping chores, like storing, copying, and deleting files. If ROM chips are the brains of a Mac or a PC, then RAM is brainpower, the receptacle into which data is written, remembered, and retrieved. In RAM you have work space to create and modify files. PRAM (pronounced pee-ram) maintains time, date, and various control panel settings and keeps track of which devices are connected to the printer and modem ports on your computer. Single in-line memory modules (SIMMS) are the package of memory chips where RAM resides within a Macintosh.

Color applications and complex software programs require increasing amounts of RAM, which is measured in megabytes (mb). A Macintosh running its operating system and Microsoft Word may require 4 mb; a PC running Windows, as much as 10 mb. The adage is true: if you can never be too thin or too rich, you also can never have enough RAM or enough storage.

Storage

When PCs and Macs first came into offices and homes, the standard hard drive held 20 mb, which was enough room to store all kinds of software and, people thought, thousands of documents. From this beginning, programs proliferated in number and all programs became feature-laden, requiring additional storage. The files produced with these programs also got bigger as graphics were added and as many early adopters switched to color. Now hard drives of 500 mb and larger are common for home office use, with the cost of storage continuing to decline dramatically.

RAM is a type of memory allocated to run the computer's system software applications, such as **QuarkXPress** for page layout, **Adobe Illustrator** for illustration, or **Claris Filemaker Pro** for database management. **RAM** is memory in action, as opposed to the static memory of hard drive storage.

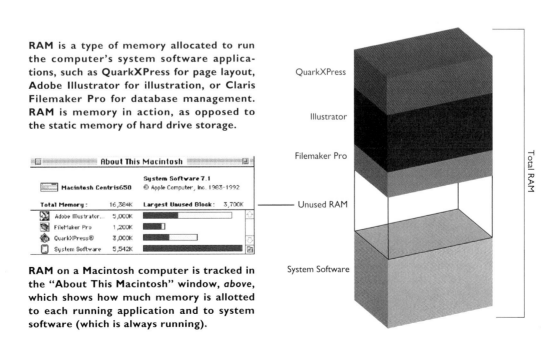

About This Macintosh

Macintosh Centris650   System Software 7.1
© Apple Computer, Inc. 1983-1992

Total Memory :	16,384K	Largest Unused Block :	3,700K
Adobe Illustrator...	5,000K		
FileMaker Pro	1,200K		
QuarkXPress®	3,000K		
System Software	5,542K		

RAM on a Macintosh computer is tracked in the "About This Macintosh" window, *above*, which shows how much memory is allotted to each running application and to system software (which is always running).

QuarkXPress

Illustrator

Filemaker Pro

Unused RAM

System Software

Total RAM

Laptop Computers

A laptop computer has become essential for journalists, sales professionals, and many other kinds of business executives, with home office use a secondary consideration to its functionality and convenience on the road. Laptop computers are also useful for the nomadic worker who works at various locations around the house, in the yard, or by the pool, as well as on the road or at a weekend retreat. PC and Macintosh systems have comparable laptop models, although the multitude of PC brands makes these models more price-competitive than Macintosh models.

Laptop computers can be configured to include a fax/modem that provides access to on-line services and can send and receive faxes. Theoretically, you can connect your laptop computer to a cellular telephone to send and receive faxes while you climb a mountain and transmit electronic mail from a canoe on a wild river in the wilderness. In real life, though, most business is conducted in officelike surroundings, and these fanciful uses remain figments of a Silicon Valley copywriter's imagination.

Speed and memory are still the critical variables for laptop computers. Battery life is important, but you may find that you only use battery power when you fly or take notes in someone else's conference room. Airlines now prohibit laptop use during take-off and landing (including an additional ten minutes at either end). A color screen will devour battery life, and most laptop users find that its benefits do not justify the additional cost.

Apple Macintosh Powerbook 180 computer.

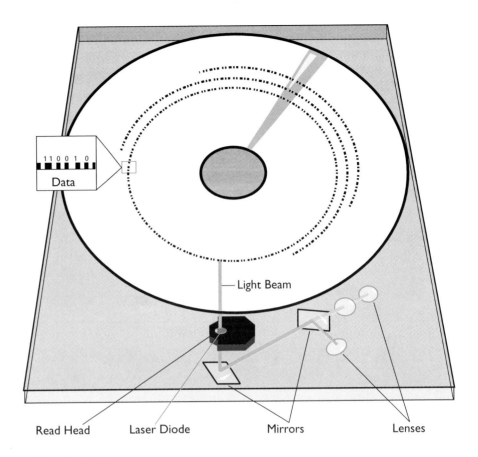

Data

Light Beam

Read Head   Laser Diode   Mirrors   Lenses

CD-ROM

For most of us, CD-ROM has not yet found its business application utility, although some specialized data retrieval is only available on CD-ROM. It has become increasingly popular as a media for educational and game software, and many home computers featured by computer supermarkets now include built-in CD-ROM players.

If your children do not use your computer and if you have no immediate use for CD-ROM technology in your work, it is probably best to spend the additional money (about $500) on software, more memory, or additional storage. You can always add a CD-ROM player later.

Power Macintosh

You can now have your cake and eat it too with the Power Macintosh, the latest generation of Macintosh computers. These can be used with the Macintosh, DOS, or Windows operating systems, and they run each of the systems at significantly faster processing speeds. While somewhat expensive, the Power Macintosh series is priced comparably with the Pentium-based PCs, the latest and fastest computers running DOS and Windows. The DOS feature on the Power Macintosh is accessible through a program from Insignia Solutions called SoftWindows, permitting the movement of text between files running on Mac, DOS, and Windows applications.

CD-ROM storage, *above*, like magnetic hard drives, contains a spiral track that begins near the center and extends to the outer edges. The light beam detects—through mirrors and lenses—digital data, which is transmitted to a read head and laser diodes before reaching your screen.

The lowest-priced personal laser printers produce four pages per minute at a resolution of 300 dpi. With something called Memory Enhancement technology, standard memory can be effectively doubled.

Printers

The current generation of desktop printers uses either inkjet or laser technology. Inkjet printers provide good quality at a moderate price; some also offer color printing. The problem with inkjet printers is that they are very slow compared with laser models.

Laser printers offer higher quality and higher speed at a higher price. If you plan to produce professional graphics, you must consider a laser printer employing Postscript technology, which will add several hundred dollars to the cost of the printer but will provide much greater functionality: it will open an array of applications and fonts that rely on Postscript technology.

Buying a Computer System

Buying a computer is somewhat more difficult than buying a car, yet the two experiences have a few things in common. Would you ask a car salesperson to teach you how to drive? While few would consider it an automobile dealership's responsibility to teach driver education, many think of a computer store as a place to learn how to operate computers.

While it is possible to find a computer salesperson who will make independent recommendations, your luck will be about as good as getting a Ford dealer to recommend a Chevy. Their job is to make a sale, and making sure you have adequate postsales support is secondary to their sales volume.

You may also purchase a computer system and software from a discount warehouse, through the mail, or from a small systems integrator. The cost will vary according to which system you choose and how much technical support and service you buy. Macintosh computers are only recently available through mail order and only a few models (the Performa series) are merchandised through big discounters such as CompUSA, Staples, and Office Depot.

In general, you should follow four basic steps when buying your first computer system:

- With advice from someone you trust (and who does not have a stake in the decision), decide which platform, Mac or PC, and your overall targeted budget.
- Check magazines, discount stores, and mail order sources to find the lowest price for the best system within your budget.
- Finally, locate an individual or small company that will sell you the equipment, install it, and provide initial technical support. The difference between their price and bottom dollar is the amount you will need to pay for support

services. Keep in mind that in the computer business, everything is negotiable and competition is fierce. Computers running DOS and Windows are increasingly considered commodities, with few differences between the brand names.

- Obtain software training from a different source, or simply buy a book or work with the user's manuals that come with the program. Training by mass-market computer dealers is notoriously overpriced and usually only marginally useful. Some manuals are good, most are not. Often a $30 book can save you an extraordinary amount of time and aggravation. Having a computer-literate friend help you through the first few days or weeks can be a godsend. Finally, make use of the software publisher's technical support line. Registered users of software usually get free technical support for a period of time. Some companies do not charge at all, while others charge after you have been using the software for ninety days or more.

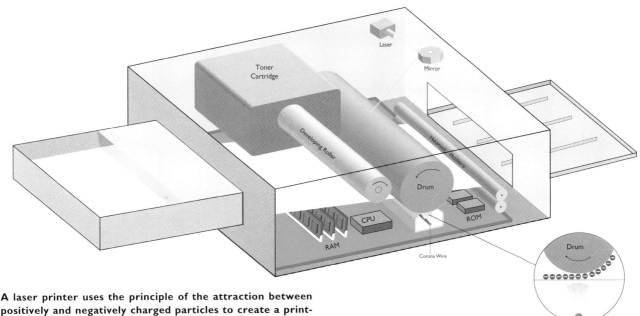

A laser printer uses the principle of the attraction between positively and negatively charged particles to create a printed page. It has a **CPU, RAM,** and **ROM** of its own, which allow it to process commands from a computer. A laser beam is aimed at a rotating drum by deflection off a polygonal mirror. The drum is coated with a light-sensitive material that reacts as the laser beam hits it, drawing toner, a fine powder, from the developing roller onto the drum. The paper pulled in from a paper tray passes between the drum and a corona wire, which is positively charged. This positive charge draws the negatively charged toner particles from the drum to the paper. The toner is bonded to the paper by passing between two heated rollers.

THE COMPLETE HOME OFFICE

Home office computer-compatible furniture is available for every budget. It can be a do-it-your-self, snap-together desk made of lightweight, scratch-resistant synthetic materials, like this one at *right*, or a piece of solid case goods costing several thousand dollars.

The WristAir 2000 Keyboard Pad from North Coast Medical is designed to help protect the wrist against cumulative trauma injuries by absorbing vibration and by supporting the wrist in the optimal position for working at a keyboard. The wrist pad is one inch thick.

Manufacturers of both computers and furniture are becoming increasingly sophisticated and sensitive to a home worker's needs, based on market research, customer feedback, and trial and error.

One problem for furniture manufacturers is to appropriately scale and configure desks and storage units. Home office units must accommodate a wide variety of computer models, printers, and peripherals, such as in the Jean Beirise Collection from Herman Miller for the Home, *above*.

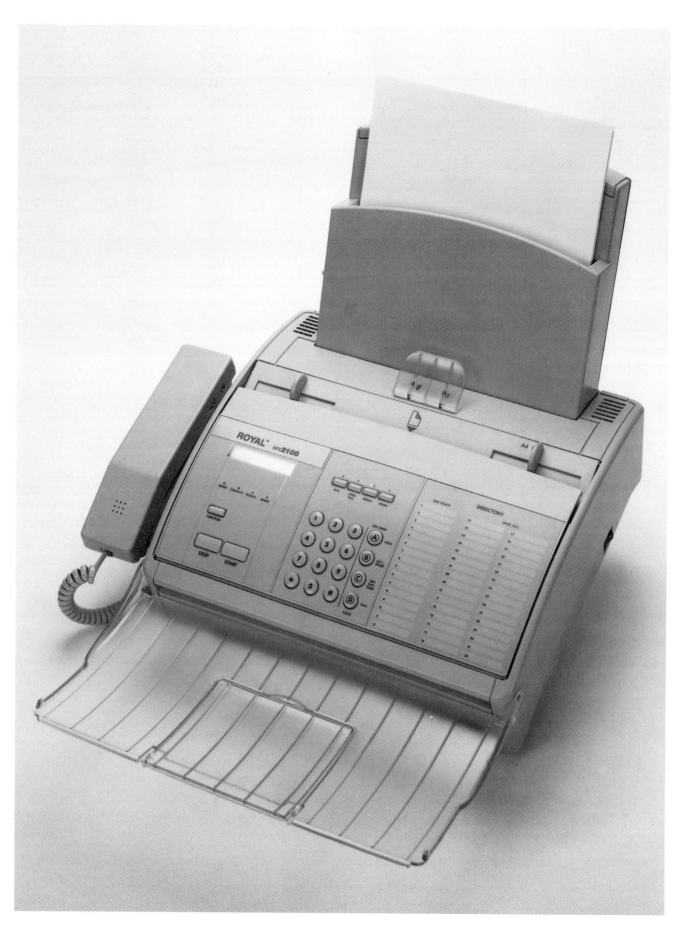

Copiers, Fax Machines, and Fax/Modems

A good copier may cost as much as or even more than your computer, depending on the features necessary for you to complete your work efficiently. If you need to copy every day, you'll need your own copier. Driving to and from a copy center is inconvenient, and the cost of such copies quickly becomes prohibitively expensive. If, for example, you bill $50 per hour, a thirty-minute round-trip to the copy shop for five copies of a two-page expense report will cost you $2.50 per page in lost income, plus the actual cost of the copies. Desktop copiers are becoming increasingly sophisticated, providing reduction and enlargement features, large paper trays, exposure control, and reasonable speed for less than $1,000. Operating these copiers is expensive on a cost-per-copy basis, but not much more than a copy service. Essentially, you are buying the convenience of having a copier handy for small jobs, but you may still need a copy service for big projects. Desktop copiers typically do not have automatic feed, two-sided copying, or sorter bins, nor do they accept ledger-sized paper (11 x 14 inches).

If these features are important to you, consider buying an office copier. There are plenty of used copiers available (businesses trade-in and trade-up all the time), but it is important to evaluate carefully the service, repair, and maintenance cycle and the financing costs. Without an annual service contract, a service call can cost $100–150, plus parts. A copier that has been well cared for may need only two service calls a year; a problem copier will need constant service. You can protect yourself to some degree by buying a used copier that carries a parts and labor warranty for ninety days or more from a firm that will provide future service.

Used copiers fall into three categories: "refurbished," "reconditioned," or "remanufactured." Refurbished machines are old machines that have been well maintained and cleaned up. Reconditioned and remanufacturered units have new parts and have been tested.

Facsimile (fax) machines have become a standard home office appliance. The value of faxing is particularly noticeable when communicating overseas. Sending a three-day express letter to Japan from the eastern United States costs $30, while an instantaneous one-page fax costs about 75 cents over AT&T phone lines.

Some fax machines store faxes so that they may be retrieved by computer from a remote site, while others can store literally hundreds of fax numbers for sending targeted mail to an entire mailing list within a few minutes or hours. The latest small office/home office fax machines are combined with a laser printer and copier. However, this sort of one-man band will leave you completely stranded if it ever breaks down. Plain paper fax machines produce high-quality copies.

Desktop copiers offer convenience for producing a single copy of a short report, or multiple copies of a single page, but are not recommended for large copying chores.

If you buy an office copy machine, it is useful to purchase a copier stand that provides storage below for supplies. Also remember that a copier, unlike a computer, requires a lot of power. A desktop copier needs more than a thousand watts during operation, and an office copier may need much more.

Facsimile (fax) machines have few working parts compared to copiers and are virtually maintenance-free. While a wide array of features is available on fax machines, most have a separate handset for voice transmission, a jack for a telephone connection, speed and memory dialing, and produce some kind of activity report. Options include sending at a preset time, sending to more than one location, sending a relay fax (assuming the recipient machine also has a relay function), confidential sending, polling (requesting documents from other fax units with polling), automatic redialing, and

memory receiving and sending. Just about all fax machines can make the occasional copy, but they're slower than copiers, and the end result isn't as crisp.

Of these optional features, memory is perhaps the most useful. A fax machine with memory will receive a fax even if it has run out of paper. It simply reads the incoming fax into memory and prints it out when you have installed more paper. If you send long documents to foreign countries, memory sending can save money: You dial a number, then send your document into memory before you are connected, transmitting it in only a fraction of the time that it takes for each page to go through when you have connected.

Plain paper fax machines use a laser rather than a thermal copy engine, providing single-sheet output rather than from a roll of thermal paper. These can also be purchased as part of a laser printer, although these all-in-one

Wired for Speed

In planning your telecom needs, remember that we are riding the crest of a wave. Twisted pair copper wire, called D-station wire, is the kind of wiring found in residences. In the near future, we may send and receive voice, video, and data signals through coaxial cable (which now provides cable television), ISDN (integrated service digital network), or fiber optics. For a few businesses (such as multimedia producers and others requiring massive carrying capacity), custom ISDN or fiber optics installations will serve high-end, high-speed data needs, but for the rest of us, off-ramps to America's data highway into our home offices are only now becoming accessible. In the future, a range of new services, from video telephone to worldwide transmission of color photographs and interactive home office shopping, will become routine.

machines often promise more than they deliver. Plain paper faxes are far superior to thermal-roll faxes, and far more expensive, costing approximately twice as much.

Fax/modems, devices that fit inside of or next to your computer, have become quite common and useful primarily for sending faxes. Sending a fax directly from your computer saves you the hassle and time of printing the document, dialing the fax number, and waiting for the fax to go through. The software that drives fax/modems can maintain a log of faxes sent, redial numbers that are busy, verify the number of pages sent, provide a variety of cover sheets, and store hundreds of fax numbers.

Fax/modems are less convenient in receiving faxes and cannot send a document that already exists as hard copy (such as a news clip). To receive a fax via your fax/modem, you must have a telephone line connected and your computer in a fax-receiving mode.

Greg Simpson took a laptop computer, with a fax/modem, along on his weekly out-of-town travels. The fax/modem was the perfect solution to sending or receiving a fax in his hotel room. He could also use it to access on-line data services to update the latest costing information from his company and check his electronic mail, all during the evening from his hotel room.

This "faxphone" contains features such as automatic paper cutting, decurling, paper saver, document feeder, one-touch dialing, and delayed transmission features.

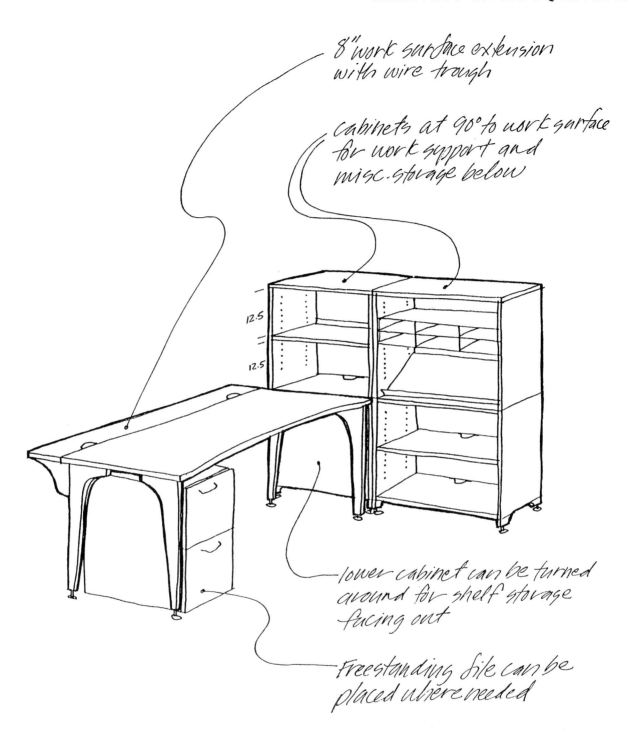

8" work surface extension with wire trough

cabinets at 90° to work surface for work support and misc. storage below

12.5

12.5

lower cabinet can be turned around for shelf storage facing out

Freestanding file can be placed where needed

The storage of equipment was a principal concern in the design of this flexible grouping from Herman Miller, *opposite*. An early preliminary concept drawing, *above*, by Coons Beirise Design shows that the cabinet grouping can be arranged in a variety of ways. The table, *foreground*, has an eight-inch surface extension and extends over a free-standing file cabinet. Storage cabinets can be stacked high or low and configured as part of a workstation or separately, unattached to the table.

Telecommunication Equipment and Services

Telecommunications strategies used in organizing your link to the outside world are perhaps one of the most important aspects of home office planning. Increasing numbers of workers are being seduced by the extraordinary promise of electronic communications from home-based and nomadic businesses. Even large corporations are beginning to "free" their employees from their desks and send them homeward with software, data files, and a modem link to their electronic mail systems. Companies are finding that working at home with the proper communication tools and equipment is almost like being at the office. Equipping your home office to optimize efficient and effective communication may become essential to your goals.

Successful home office communication strategies can handle anything that a small business office can handle. Indeed, the major market for office communications equipment is now called "SOHO," for "small office/ home office," the two now becoming synonymous to the trade.

In addition to modular telephone jacks (RJ11 plugs), you may also need wiring for Ethernet or other connectors to network your computers and printers. To plan a system effectively, you might need to hire a consultant who provides cabling services for offices and who can help integrate your home and office telecom wiring into a single system. A home office installation may require two voice lines, additional lines for data and fax, and a home line, for a total of five phone lines. You may also wish to wire for one or two lines that remain unconnected until you need additional service.

Although a single line with a fax/phone switch is practical for many home offices, your phone line will be tied up when you are sending or receiving a fax, a distinct problem for those business communications that require sending a document during the course of a call. A second or third line also permits an electronic mail or on-line

hookup always to be ready, so you can send or receive electronic mail messages while the telephone is in use. With more than one person working in a home office, the need for phone lines seems to grow exponentially.

Telephone companies have differing and changing policies about residential and business services. In many jurisdictions, residential service is defined simply by the location of the service, regardless of its use for business or personal calls. Other services may have policies based on use or some combination of use and location. In any event, these services and policies will soon change as nearly all local phone companies enter into competition with cable, long distance, and even power companies.

Telecom cabling is not difficult or particularly expensive. The trick is to find someone experienced in home installations who will know how to lay wires along moldings and snake them through drywall. It's easiest to find these consultants through someone who sells computer equipment for a living. Finally, it is best to locate your modular jacks after you have settled on a furniture plan and computer system placement.

Made of Lucite, this phone stand seems to disappear on a desk, and it provides space for a message pad beneath.

The AT&T Cordless Intercom/Speakerphone features a handset and base, both with built-in dial pads. The base has a speakerphone, so calls can be made from either unit. The phone can be operated up to 1,000 feet away from the base in ideal conditions.

Telephone Equipment

You can buy telephones, services, or some combination thereof to get what you need. As with office location, family and business telephone setups can be a bad mix. Full-time home office workers will need a two-line telephone (even if they also have "call waiting") to set up conference calls and to make calls on one line while another is on hold. To receive personal calls in a home office, it is relatively easy to install a home phone line as the second line on the office telephone, each having a distinctive ring (as a feature of two-line telephones).

The features on AT&T, Panasonic, and other two-line telephones are similar: hold and conferencing buttons, last-number redial, speakerphone, volume controls, and memory dialing.

Beyond the telephone instrument itself, there are answering machines, modems, fax/modems, fax-to-phone switches, and a wide range of specialty equipment. If you use the phone all day, a telephone headset helps avoid neck strain and permits you to move around more, with both hands free to make notes using your keyboard. Generally, headsets connect to an amplifier that connects to your telephone, which needs to be off the hook while you are using it. Useful features include a quick disconnection so that you can go fetch a file without removing the headset, a long cord, and a mute button so that you can have a private side conversation while on the phone. If your workplace is noisy (perhaps you're playing music when the phone rings), you may opt for a headset that covers both ears. If you wish to roam around your office as you speak, cordless sets are available at about twice the cost of conventional models.

More important than the equipment you buy are the services that you select, which often will cost as much or more each month as hardware that will last for years.

Telephone Services

Your local phone company, its regional affiliate, or a long distance carrier will offer a varied mix of convenient services. Not all of these services are available in every region, and not all of them are marketed under these names, but most are available in many places.

- *Answer Call:* a voice mail service that in some systems provides two messages: one for when you are away and one for when you are on the phone—a service not available from a regular answering machine. *Answer Call* also has the convenience of remote access, thirty to forty-five minutes of message storage, and a reminder that lets you call in several messages to yourself (such as your wedding anniversary or mother's birthday) and then rings you up on the appointed day.

- *True Connections* from AT&T, also called *EasyReach*: a "portable" long distance number where you may be reached wherever you are. As you move from home office to car to hotel room to vacation home, you dial in a code from any phone and those with your 500 number can reach you as you roam. Options include reverse billing for callers that you select and call forwarding. Your assigned 500 number will stay with you for life. In the near future, *Personal Communication Systems*, a new wireless technology that will compete with cellular telephones, will provide similar services.

- *Call Waiting:* the most common special service, but a headache for a busy office. Incoming calls interrupt the call that you are on.
- *Call Return:* lets you know the number of the last person who called you by dialing a code and receiving the number by recorded message.
- *Caller ID:* a device that gives you the telephone number of every incoming call. It also blocks your number from being given to another phone with Caller ID.
- *Call Forwarding:* allows you to send incoming calls to any number you choose. You can also set up telephone numbers in other cities with *Remote Call Forwarding*, routing the calls to your phone.
- *Call Screen* or *Call Blocking* (different names for the same service): permit you to reject up to ten phone numbers (with a message indicating that the calls are blocked from the calling number).
- *Three-Way Calling* can be arranged for those without a two-line phone.
- *Repeat Dialing* doesn't tie up your phone line while you continue to dial a busy number.

Some of these services are available as features of the telephone instrument itself rather than an additional service that you purchase. Many two-line telephones, for instance, have a conferencing feature and last-number redial.

A two-line remote answering machine, with dual microcassette system that answers calls on both lines, is useful if you have more than one phone line that callers can use. Other features include voice help menu, selective playback, call intercept, toll saver, and a play-new-messages-only option.

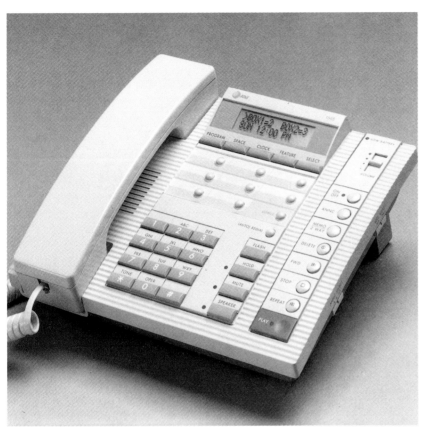

This telephone answering system from **AT&T** features a voice mailbox which gives users the ability to record messages in four different "mailboxes." It also allows you to present more than one announcement to callers and permits up to 26 minutes of recording time.

Long Distance Services

Long distance services can be divided into billing schemes and convenience services. Billing and pricing schemes are market-driven; they change constantly as various long distance carriers and wholesalers compete with each other to capture a greater market share. The most common offerings from these companies are incoming and outgoing toll-free 800 number services; base minimum rates and installation charges keep diminishing as competition remains heated. Outgoing 800 service is simply a discounted long distance service that averages the per-minute or per-second charges over all domestic calls, and provides a set rate per minute or hour for use. Incoming 800 services, popular with businesses seeking to expand their market, provide a convenient way for customers to call without being charged for a long distance call.

AT&T retains about half of the long distance service in the United States; MCI, Sprint, and dozens of smaller carriers divide the other half. Since the quality of a call can vary by service or area, it is a matter of trial and error to determine which of the long distance services is better on the basis of line quality.

It is also impossible to compare costs accurately, since billing schemes are constantly changing and cost comparisons are invariably skewed. One way to save money is to order your long distance service through a long distance broker, a business that simply provides sales and billing services. Long distance telephone service brokers are often listed under telephone communication services in your yellow pages directory.

Elizabeth Haskell was happy with her service from AT&T, but was told by a friend that she could receive substantially lower rates by ordering the service through a broker. She contacted a broker in her area and found that she could retain her AT&T services, including the same phone and credit card numbers, for about 20 percent less per call.

Greg Simpson often wants to discuss new projects with two or three colleagues located in different cities. Since it's usually impractical or impossible to get everyone together in one location, he sets up an electronic meeting with his long-distance teleconferencing service. For this service he pays a per-minute and per-location charge plus "bridge" charges, which are relatively expensive but much cheaper than airfare and taxicabs.

Home Office Strategy: International Understanding

One truly exotic and invaluable service offered by AT&T is called Language Line, which provides translator services in more than 140 languages and costs $3 to 4 per minute, a remarkably good buy.

Over the past two years, I have worked with a major client in Tokyo, Japan. Although a member of his staff is fluent in English, I have occasionally needed to communicate with suppliers and other Tokyo offices.

For both AT&T subscribers and nonsubscribers, the service is available 24 hours a day, 365 days a year and can be charged to your credit card. The service works in one of two ways: if you want to begin the call with an interpreter on the line, you call the AT&T Language Line and they will place your call. If you have a two-line phone with conferencing capability, you can place the call that you have made on hold, then call Language Line and conference in the translator. It takes a few minutes to set up the service the first time you try it, so it is wise to make the arrangements before placing the call. You can also use the service for domestic calling to talk with someone who speaks a language that you don't.

This headset telephone combines headset and cordless phone in a single product. The headset plugs into the cordless handset, and the handset is carried in a special leather "glove" that clips to your belt.

On-line Services

Electronic mail has become routine for large corporations but is only now becoming convenient and useful for independent home office workers. Computer-generated on-line services provide a means to transmit messages and documents instantaneously around the world without long distance charges. They also provide an amazing variety of information—both for free and with connect charges—including airline schedules, library catalogs, weather reports, movie reviews, stock quotations, special interest forums, and information from literally thousands of sources. Using software provided by the on-line service, a modem, and your computer, these services charge a monthly subscription fee (usually less than $10) and provide documentation of your usage, regular mailings, and free telephone or fax help lines.

There is a confusing array of routine and exotic ways to manage and enhance telecommunications. You can choose on-line services from CompuServe, Prodigy, Dow Jones, and America Online; long distance services; services from regional Bell operating companies; and new dial-up services from cable television providers. How you select and use these services, both separately and together, will greatly add to or detract from your home office productivity.

Greg Simpson suddenly lost his job when his company consolidated sales regions. Instead of scouring the Sunday classifieds and sending out hundreds of résumés, he used CompuServe and America Online as a key part of his job search. He scrutinized the dozens of electronic "forums" available on the systems and found one whose purpose was to put high-tech sales professionals in contact with each other, to be a sounding board for ideas, and to provide an ideal environment for networking. He was pleased that key people in several companies responded to ideas he transmitted to the forum. He started communicating regularly with the regional sales manager of one firm, and after three months, he was offered a new job.

Jim Forrest used CompuServe, Dow Jones News Retrieval, and other on-line services to get critically important business information: corporate financial statements, security prices, Wall Street analysts' reports, up-to-the-minute news on the companies and industries he focused on, digests of articles in business journals, federal and state regulations affecting industry and commerce, congressional testimony by industry lobbyists, Federal Reserve actions, economists' interpretations of the latest economic indicators, international financial and political developments, and myriad other information on all the business topics he had to track each day.

Jim estimated that before he started using on-line services, he spent five to ten hours a week scouring newspapers and trade journals to find this information. He was certain he missed two-thirds of it, and what he did find was often dated and useless. On-line services typically provide current-day, and in some cases up-to-the-minute information. Jim got this current awareness by spending an hour a week on-line.

America Online (AOL) is a popular general interest on-line service, offering such publications as *Time, Atlantic Monthly,* and the *Chicago Tribune* online, as well as a broad spectrum of other information. AOL is distinguished by its graphical user interface and its easy hookup to the Internet.

CompuServe, Inc. is another general interest on-line system that offers a basic service for a monthly fee, as well as premium services for additional hourly charges. The basic service includes e-mail, news, sports, reference publications, shopping, financial data, travel, entertainment, and games. Special interest forums allow you to share ideas with people around the world.

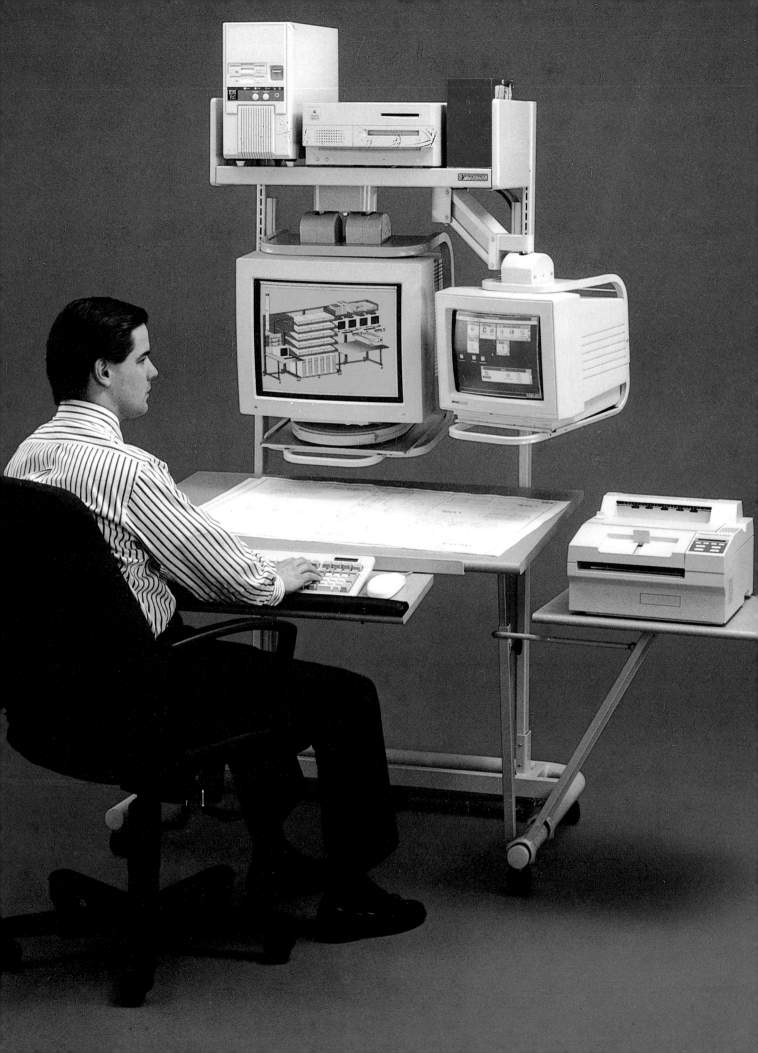

It is apparent from all indications that on-line services, two-way telecommunications, teleconferencing, video-conferencing, walk-around personal systems, and the expansion and improvements in cellular phones and beepers will dramatically affect the way we do business in home offices.

Every big company in the world involved in telecommunications, movies and other entertainment, publishing, cable, and broadcasting are scrambling to define a marketplace that theoretically will funnel our every communication need for family and work through a single pipe into our living rooms and home offices, providing a bewildering array of services.

The problems are ones of content, cost, and commitment. New basic services will be delivered enmass to consumers as quality increases and prices fall. Because the technology is well ahead of the imaginations of those who produce content, it will probably take a long time for truly new communications methods to fully penetrate the home office. Instead, equipment and services should simply get better, cheaper, more easily available, and, we hope, more understandable to more people.

For the true techie, the Ergotron offers a streamlined, all-purpose Design Workcenter. Ergotron products provide a variety of ways to integrate computer equipment with office systems manufactured by major companies such as Herman Miller or Steelcase, or with more individualized office environments.

The key benefit of an Ergotron system is that it removes computer equipment and wiring from the desktop either by hanging components, usually monitors, on retractable arms or by providing holders, trolleys, shelves, trays, and caddies for CPUs and other computer components.

CHAPTER 5
THE HOME OFFICE
OF THE FUTURE

The home office movement is a natural consequence of the transition from an economy based on the manufacture and distribution of materials to one based on the manipulation and transmittal of information. America's "information economy," which was predicted by Daniel Bell and Alvin Toffler two decades ago, relies on smaller businesses and individual entrepreneurs to cultivate a demand for niche products and services in a global marketplace. These businesses and services are increasingly home-based, as communications and other technologies begin to eliminate the differences between home-based work and work performed in a commercial office.

With this specialized nature of tasks and the knowledge needed to perform them, it has become more important for workers to be near their data than it is to be near their colleagues. But in practice they still need to be in instant contact with both.

The Burdick Group of furniture by Herman Miller was designed to create different work zones for writing, reading, meeting, or communicating, with these work zones arranged for the individual worker to maximize the work process.

The Home Office in the Information Economy

The information economy predicted two decades ago and now heralded by Peter Drucker and Robert Reich has become, in effect, a small business economy. Indeed, all net growth in employment in the United States in the past two decades has come from small business. The total employment of firms having more than 5,000 employees was higher in 1970 than today; meanwhile, total U.S. employment has increased by 50 percent. Even within large businesses, the scale of operations has become radically smaller, as big corporations are restructured into ever more compact working groups. As businesses decentralize, smaller offices give way to home and "virtual" offices—that is, offices in a briefcase containing simply a laptop computer, a pocket pager, and a cellular telephone.

Until recently, the information economy relied on large-scale organizations that operated mainframe computers programmed and maintained by highly skilled, highly specialized workers. These organizations kept data entry separate from data processing, and both were under the watchful, even dictatorial eye of a centralized management information services department. When microcomput-

A Techline home office, *above*, combines freestanding furniture components with other elements that can be wall-mounted. Techline furniture is particularly well-suited for designers and knowledge workers who use a large number of computer components and peripherals; it can be configured to provide a nearly limitless amount of surface area.

Small, specialized computers such as this language translator, *opposite top,* or spell checker, *opposite bottom,* both from Seiko, are considerably smaller and less expensive than laptop computers but have a limited range of functions. Typically, these types of devices are used for address files and as calendars, in addition to single-purpose models such as those pictured.

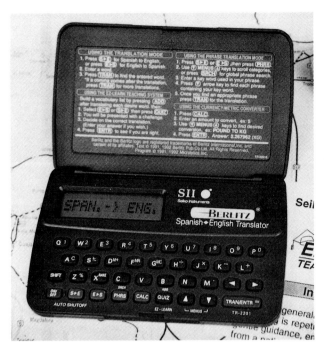

ing came to the office, it first was linked to a central mainframe to access large databases and for electronic mail. As microprocessing and mass storage systems became cheaper and faster, the industry devoted to developing and maintaining mainframe computing began to wither. Now microcomputing and related technologies are growing exponentially in the number of home offices across America.

Cheap Thrills

A leading cause of the wholesale switch to microcomputers is the phenomenal decline in the cost of computing. Using the standard measure of *millions of instructions per second* (MIPS), in 1980, the cost for 4.5 MIPS was $4.5 million; in 1990, was $100,000; and by the year 2000, will be $10,000.

Faster computers and more powerful software are replacing production workers; voice mail is replacing the receptionist. Intuit's Quicken, a widely used, simplified accounting software package, is replacing the bookkeeper. Office hours are becoming more flexible. More time is spent actually doing the work, less time is spent directing others. Freelancers, part-time workers, contractors, suppliers, vendors, and consultants are hired as the need arises, communicating through fax, electronic mail, and phone from (often) far-flung corners of the globe. Time

zones seem to be the only variable between business a mile away or three thousand miles away.

The question is whether large businesses and major corporations, labor unions, and government will accept the home office trend. Many argue that it simply will not happen, given managers' natural inclination to control staff—a difficulty with home-based employees.

Perhaps more important is the culture of big business and the tendency to devote large parts of the working day to meetings. Looking into the soul of management, one discovers the importance of person-to-person contacts in decision-making processes at high levels. On a more practical level, large businesses, law firms, banks, and government agencies love the prestige of their downtown locations, and the importance of their fixed real estate assets in central business districts to their balance sheets cannot be overlooked. They would also argue that proximity to ancillary business services and a number of suppliers is essential, as is the vertical integration of technology made possible by skyscrapers. It is much simpler to lay cable that networks computers and provides fiber optics in tall buildings than it is in apartments and homes throughout a region.

Whatever the preferences of big-business managers, home offices are the wave of the future. Some large firms have adopted interim policies. AT&T, for example, organized a Telecommuting Office Center in Manhattan, replacing three sales offices in New York and New England

Bradley Rytz, of San Francisco, designed this small home office, with a custom-made curved desk facing a deck and a desert landscape beyond.

Customized office furniture is an attractive option for home offices that occupy irregular or unusual spaces that may have a low, sloped ceiling, non-right angles, or simply extremely tight space. Creative solutions provided by architects or interior designers are not always more expensive than store-bought furniture, particularly if the elements are constructed on-site by carpenters, rather than in a shop by a cabinetmaker.

The problem with customization is not so much the cost as the ability of the designer to anticipate the full range of uses and functionality of the home office: Computer and telecommunications equipment will probably be changed more frequently than the furniture it rests on. As a conse-

quence, a custom desk and shelving system can quickly outlive its usefulness, as home office workers become more sophisticated in the use of technology or as their needs change.

The advantage of purchasing standard furniture components is the greater possibility that they can accommodate a variety of equipment choices, based on often extensive market research and testing. Consider, for example, a computer printer of the late 1980s. These devices were substantially larger, heavier, more expensive, and slower than they are today. A home office worker of 1989 would have likely replaced such a printer with something better by now, requiring some adjustment in desk surface arrangement. New desking and storage systems are increasingly "computer-literate" as the marketplace becomes more sophisticated.

and reducing its total square footage of expensive office space by two-thirds. The permanent staff was reduced from 300 to 50, but an additional 65 workstations were set up to accommodate visiting employees who otherwise work from home offices or on the road. Ernst & Ernst, the accounting Goliath, adopted a similar strategy, reducing its office space around the country by one million square feet and providing "concierge" services and temporary offices for its nomadic auditors.

Even the federal government is experimenting with its Federal Alternate Worksite Center (patterned after state government projects in Hawaii and Washington). The first federal center, located seventy-five miles from Washington in Hagerstown, Maryland, provides electronic mail, high-speed data transmission lines, computer workstations, meeting rooms, and other facilities for workers who drive to the center daily, or who work from home offices and use the center for meetings, downloading files, or other high-tech clerical chores.

While the reluctance of management is one obstacle for some workers craving a home office of their own, other workers are themselves reluctant to become telecommuters. According to the *Wall Street Journal*, Apple Computer expected to be "inundated with requests" from workers who wanted to be considered for a pilot program, but instead received fewer than half the number they anticipated. Some people do not have an agreeable place to establish a proper home office. In New York, for example, apartments are often too small. Some suburbanites cannot manage a sensible workday with small children at home, while others use their downtown office to escape the stress at home.

For other employees, working away from the action or out on the fringe is also threatening: they believe that proximity to the center of power is a prerequisite for advancement. Many also feel that face-to-face interaction with their colleagues is essential for their work. Lawyers and advertising executives, for example, are two categories of professionals who have resisted decentralization because they fear the loss of camaraderie and cohesion, and worry that someone else will appropriate their clients.

Along with personal computing, telecommunications will play an increasingly important role in the growth of home offices over the next decade. Until recently, only large businesses and universities had the capacity for high-speed data transmission for information retrieval, electronic mail, and conferencing. This is undergoing tremendous change and is permitting networking among computers without respect to their physical location. This advancing electronic interconnectedness among business offices across cities, mountains, and oceans is moving at an extraordinary pace. Networking is expanding as capacity increases and as fiber optics, ISDN (integrated service digital network), and satellite transmission become universal in business communications, whether at a central location or from a home office. Hardware continues to evolve into smaller, faster, and less expensive configurations. Software is evolving into the realm of artificial intelligence, providing a seamless interface between user and computer, offering sophisticated information processing without requiring specific expert knowledge of the computer's operations.

This inexpensive electronic organizer with 18K memory, *above*, can store up to 700 items such as names, addresses, and telephone and fax numbers.

Herman Miller's Equa chair beside a Scooter stand, *opposite*.

Decentralization and the Home Office

The proliferation of home offices is simply one of many symptoms of a decentralized society. Its effect can be seen everywhere as people move their work and homes from center cities to city perimeters; as people move from large cities to small towns, suburbs, and the country; as people move from the Northeast and Midwest to the South and Southwest, and from California to the intermountain and western states.

Decentralization means that large corporations are downsizing to medium- and small-sized businesses. Small working units are carved out of large businesses, each operating autonomously from separate offices (or even no office at all), from different regions of the country and from different parts of the world. It means that corporations increasingly outsource and subcontract services and employ contingent workers, forming strategic alliances and temporary, informal cooperative relationships to perform tasks that were previously performed only by employees.

Decentralization means that corporations rely less on hierarchical decision-making and more on consensus decision-making, and use labor-management cooperative arrangements, quality circles, smaller networks, and less formal structures. Decentralization means that companies use technology—including electronic mail, video conferencing, networked telecommunications, and personal computers (with less reliance on mainframe processing)—to distribute information within the corporation and to and from its customers and suppliers. (Incidentally, the trend toward a reliance on home offices by professional workers in business and technology has parallels in other parts of society. There is an American movement, called "agrophilia" by landscape historian J. B. Jackson, blooming in pastoral suburbs and the countryside, places now considered by a growing number of heretofore dedicated city dwellers as pleasant and respectable, even desirable, places to live.)

Following the decentralization trend, home offices are becoming more and more practical. The ambience, protocol, and routines of home office work are beginning to earn respect as gains in productivity over conventional office settings are reported. In studies conducted by AT&T, Pacific Telesis, Herman Miller, and others, worker satisfaction and productivity increase substantially in home office environments.

The **Geneva Task Light** provides diffused lighting that can be easily positioned for individual workstations, *below*. **Techline** office, *left*, offers wide-open surfaces and substantial cabinet and file storage.

Melinda Davidson had a part-time designer working for her in her home office. In addition to designing, her assistant handled most of the administrative, marketing, and production chores in the office. Melinda realized that a large part of her time had been devoted to such tasks when she worked for her old company and was convinced that her home office not only gave her more productive hours (since she didn't have to commute) but also the ability to make each hour more productive.

Most often people talk about their fear of isolation and their lack of self-discipline as the main problems of home office work, yet these issues tend to fade as people adjust to their new surroundings and patterns of work. Many home office workers find that face-to-face communications are less necessary than they thought. Transactions that once required in-person exchange—manager to worker, worker to customer, customer to service provider—are rapidly being replaced by asymmetrical, nonsynchronous communication. "Telephone tag" is an example. When a caller leaves a message on someone's voice mail, it is answered back to the caller's voice mail, which, in turn, is replied to without the parties ever speaking directly to one another. Managers no longer depend on secretaries to take dictation; shorter, less frequent meetings are often more productive; voice mail has become ubiquitous; telecommunications, electronic mail, pagers, and other electronic devices replace the need for many people to actually be in the office.

New Services

The road signs along America's data highway are already being posted, even though many of its special attractions have not yet been built. Most of these will be tailored to home office needs. A promising early entry are the business-to-business shopping services that let you order business services, newsletters, office supplies and furniture, computer equipment, and software on-line. Data services will become faster and easier to use, with interactive interfaces that permit powerful searching, selecting, and retrieving the information you need.

Computer, telecommunications, and news and entertainment industries are forming alliances to plan new strategies for the evolving digital age. One technological breakthrough likely to happen soon is the compression of signals sufficient to provide video phones and conferencing from our computer screen at affordable rates.

The new world of telecommunications may soon see cable television companies offering local phone services and phone companies offering pay-per-view movies. The diversity of the competing companies, the range and sophistication of services, and their cost are likely to change radically as we move into the next century.

For the telecommuter, the future may be now. Centrex services, ISDN, Switch 56, Frame Relay, and other high-tech telecommunications strategies found in corporate offices and military installations are now coming into the home, providing network speeds over long distances for voice, data, and video transmission. These strategies are closely tied to mobile business strategies and other advanced work cultures. In the future, notebook, laptop, and palmtop computers and personal digital assistants will provide wireless electronic mail, calendar synchronization, order entry, and various rapid recall and data service applications for the home-based mobile worker.

A wireless headset from Hello Direct, *left,* is useful for those home office workers who either like to move about as they talk on the phone or, more often, are typing with both hands as they take information by phone and also wish to avoid being tethered by a phone cord as they work.

The Virtual Office

Some telecommuters and other home office workers—salespeople and consultants, for example—are away from their office as much as they are in it. Workplace trends suggest that many people can do their work almost anywhere, in "virtual offices," carrying their equipment with them.

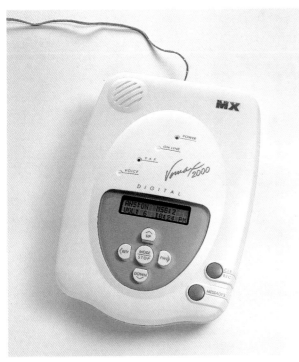

The mobile office worker with a virtual corporation is rarely in the same location as her office equipment. There are a variety of services and devices that can be programmed to move with you, forwarding voice and fax messages to designated phone numbers or fax machines at other locations. The Vomax voice and fax mail system, *above*, can be used for either voice mail or faxes.

One person's home office may be another's office away from home. Salespeople, consultants, auditors, and others who spend most of their working hours in other people's offices may hire an employee to hold down the home office while the boss goes out to work with clients. Cellular phones, beepers, personal digital assistants, and laptop and palmtop computers are part of the arsenal of roving home office workers maximizing their efficiency.

Some computers have docking stations where a laptop computer fits into a desktop computer set-up, with a full-sized keyboard and monitor, and ports to connect a CD-ROM, additional hard drive, or scanner. Other laptops are designed to work with a separate monitor, without a docking station.

Cellular telephones are available with a wide variety of features and prices. The car phone is less expensive and more powerful than a walk-around phone, and in some markets is virtually given away if you sign-up for a year's worth of connection services. A battery-powered phone that you can use outside your car (but with a cigarette-lighter attachment to power while you are driving) has less range and is more expensive, but can be used anywhere that the cellular system's signal will reach, but with a much weaker signal.

Newer mobile communication equipment will be overtaking these introductory devices as telecommunication transmission, hardware, and software converge. According to the Gartner Group, rapid technological advances will enable many new kinds of mobile computing devices to emerge in the next few years. Indeed, we now can download data from some airport pay phones, and have many new telecommunication options at hotels that cater to business travelers. As this trend continues, the links between hotel and airport, home office and corporate headquarters, businesses and individuals will become seamlessly joined.

The Worker Left Out in the Cold

For some, the transition to a home office is a transition to no office at all. Many corporations have eliminated desk space for their sales personnel, forcing workers out the door and into the field, supplying laptop computers, cellular telephones, and pagers to provide a link back to headquarters. The problem with many of these arrangements is that some salespeople require office space in which to plan campaigns, trade information with their fellow salespeople, prepare correspondence and proposals, and meet with customers. Without corporate office space, many of those in sales who are used to face-to-face encounters with the leaders of their company begin to feel cast aside.

Some companies recognize that they can easily go too far. For home office-based employees who perform desk work, communication back to a commercial office can be strong, with phone, fax, and data lines throbbing with activity all day. For the employee on the road, at a client's office, on an airplane, or on the street, the connections are more tenuous and harder to maintain. For these workers, a home office as a place to use the phone and do paperwork does not often have all of the built-in advantages other home office workers enjoy. With no routine, or an irregular one, some of the benefits of home-based work are lost. While other workers may need to transfer information between laptop and desktop computers, the traveling worker has less opportunity to use a desktop computer and is more likely to rely on a laptop for everything.

Virtual offices may be the wave of the future, but they are no substitute for a place of our own, to store information that helps us with our work, to provide familiar surroundings that improve efficiency and stimulate creativity. At best, virtual offices force us to better define our tasks so that we won't waste time performing activities peripheral to our mission. At worst, virtual offices are the equivalent of banishment, leaving workers who are often the lifeline of a corporation literally out in the cold.

The Anywhere, Anytime Office

As we look toward the future, it may be important to remember that all of the new high-powered multimedia tools and whiz-bang software actually have very little to do with the mental processes that lead us to workable and even brilliant solutions to problems. Ultimately, there is only our creativity and abilities.

For many kinds of work, the commercial office is not conducive to creative thinking. Large businesses that must constantly produce new ideas—such as advertising agencies—have experimented with study rooms and think tanks, gardens, exercise areas, and swimming pools to promote a more relaxed environment for thinking. Chiat/Day, a bicoastal advertising agency, created an office on a campus/classroom model, a mix of spaces where one can gather with others or be alone, where equipment can be moved around or taken home. The Chiat/Day office is better thought of not as an office but as a style of work. Portable or cellular phones, laptop computers, and other movable equipment now stay with the worker rather than on a desk, so tools are always handy. Hours are flexible, with some Chiat/Day employees dividing their time between home, car, office, co-worker's home, client's office, restaurant, or beach.

This concept—that work is a state of mind rather than a place to go—is revolutionizing American business. The home office is simply one piece of a larger scheme in which thought, study, and communication are liberated from the confines of rigid schedules, impersonal office decor, dress codes, and managerial politics. In this new environment, work and leisure become blurred. According to Paul Saffo, who thinks about virtual offices from his post at the Institute for the Future in Menlo Park, California, "Heaven is the anywhere, anytime office, while hell is the everywhere, everytime office."

The Rubbermaid "seat desk," one of many specialized accessories for the virtual office, provides space for files, notebooks, a clipboard for taking notes at gridlocked intersections, a calculator, pens and pencils, and other office supplies. One feature is a file bin that holds up to twenty-five letter-sized hanging files with a carrying handle for removing the file bin from the car.

THE COMPLETE HOME OFFICE

HERMAN MILLER FOR THE HOME

SLIGH FURNITURE COMPANY

TURNSTONE

HOME/ SUITE/ OFFICE···2000

TECHLINE FROM MARSHALL ERDMAN & ASSOCIATES

CHAPTER 6
FIVE HOME OFFICE
FURNITURE SOLUTIONS

America's office furniture industry recently has turned its attention to the home office, creating a new niche that combines the look and feel of residential furniture with the functionality of commercial office systems. Of the five cases first presented here, three companies—Herman Miller, Steelcase, and Sligh—have been in the office furniture business for many years. Techline has served the cross-over market of systems that can be used in either home or office. Joan Eisen, by contrast, is an interior designer who has recently designed and manufactured her own line of home office furniture.

The resources that follow present a selection of American companies that serve the small office/home office market, offering a wide range of products and services for home-based businesses and telecommuters.

Home Officing at Herman Miller

As the company that introduced modern furniture into the American home in the 1930s, Herman Miller, in Zeeland, Michigan, is no stranger to the residential environment, although it has not produced furniture for the home market for over a generation.

The Herman Miller home office team is a breed apart, a small unit that marches to the beat of a different drummer within a vast company. In fact, the home office team at Herman Miller is isolated from the rest of the company in a building that used to be a chair manufacturing facility. "The definition of the home is changing," suggested Marc Lohela, head of the home office team. "As global competition now drives our standard of living, Americans are seeking greater choice and freedom in their lives." Lohela explained that it's not so much that Herman Miller seeks to design offices for homes as it is engaged in redesigning products for the home that accommodate new styles of living and working. The principal question for Herman Miller research was to discover the nature of work outside the office environment that would provide clues to the best solutions for home offices.

The development center for Herman Miller's new home officing business is located behind their Phoenix furniture facility, one of seemingly dozens of Miller buildings scattered across the western Michigan landscape. Contemplating the function, shape, scale, and style of their home officing solutions, the Miller team first conducted extensive field research, led by Jim Long, who studied the physical environment in which people worked, their household circumstances, their organizational culture, and work group dynamics. His thirty-one study subjects, all working within four large corporations, were divided into three groups and were provided with either large-scale Herman Miller office systems, off-the-shelf office furniture of various configurations and quality levels purchased at local stores, or prototype furniture created by Miller designers for home office use. One worker whose home office had consisted of a series of television trays was provided with a large aqua metal receptionist workstation that was installed in his living room. Other solutions were, presumably, more conventional.

After six months, Jim interviewed each of the workers at the test sites, discovering how people worked at home and the points of tension created by living and working under a single roof. He discovered that most of the sites used separate (rather than shared) space for home officing, with the majority located in spare bedrooms.

A striking problem that research highlighted was the diversity of architecture and what Long called the "idiosyncrasies of the macro-geography of the home," conditions quite unlike those found in modern office buildings that are designed to enclose large uninterrupted spaces. The Miller research team confirmed what might have been obvious—dwellings are not at all suited to conventional office solutions: the scale is wrong; commercial buildings have much higher ceilings and larger expanses. Styling requirements are also completely different: most modern office furniture is not compatible with residential settings. Other factors depended on the character of the household (the presence of children, owners versus renters, the stability of the household, the permanence of the worker's work-at-home status). The age, gender, career status, and job description of the worker, as well as the region of the country, were also important factors in determining preferences for home office solutions.

In every case, the researchers found a general lack of planning in how home office solutions were selected. They concluded that people simply do not have ade-

The TD Collection is a system of home office components developed by Herman Miller after extensive research and testing. It is shown here in the Manhattan apartment of a sales executive, *opposite* and *below.*

quate sources of information to help them make sensible choices in planning, designing, and configuring a home office.

According to Long's findings, home office workers' first concern was their connection to the outside world. For corporate employees participating in the Herman Miller test, this presumably began with their ability to send and receive electronic mail to and from their colleagues, and extended to local and long distance telephone services, fax access, courier services, sending and receiving mail, and related services.

The second concern of the test subjects was surface space, followed by a desire for adequate storage. Women workers (there were thirteen in the study) were concerned about safety and security, particularly about receiving visitors in their home office when they were alone in their home. Aesthetics, including the appropriateness of office furniture in the home, was not a high priority.

On the basis of extensive in-depth interviews with people setting up home offices, the Herman Miller research team made the following conclusions about corporate workers seeking to develop a home office:

• They would benefit from design and planning assistance.
• They appreciated simplicity in approaches to home office design and layout.
• They would seek systems that were readily available and easy to install, and had technical support available in their companies for help in installation.
• They wanted home offices with comprehensive storage.
• They wanted office furniture that had large work surfaces; was safe, affordable, and expandable; and could function in a variety of situations.

The bias of the Herman Miller study was toward individual employees of medium to large organizations, generally working in middle managerial and technical positions. The study assumed that responses by self-employed, contract, and freelance workers would be similar to corporate employees and that other factors—gender, location, career stage, age, and issues relating to functionality—were more important than the source of income or the compensation of the worker. Multiperson home-based businesses were also not part of the study, nor was specific consideration given to home office workers seeking to build a new space or to reconfigure an existing space through renovation or new construction.

A Relay table by Herman Miller, *above*, is designed to fit neatly into a corner of a room or as a component in a desk configuration.

A comfortable, attractively designed home office, such as the one, *opposite*, using a Herman Miller TD Collection home office system, is conducive to efficient work. The easel is a principal component of the TD collection, as a place for an opened dictionary, important papers, or other current work. The storage system hides a computer printer, files, and shelves for supplies.

The Scooter stand, *opposite, top* and *bottom right,* was designed by Jack Kelley for Herman Miller. It serves a variety of tasks, including use as a keyboard tray, a book or music stand, or a temporary movable writing desk. A Proper chair, *opposite, bottom left,* is constructed of oval tubing for use as a lightweight, comfortable side chair that can be stacked.

Miller invited a number of furniture designers to participate in the study, providing a wide range of solutions in the form of prototypes. Through trial and error, worker feedback, and considerations relating to engineering practicality, cost, and convenience, the prototypes tested were further developed. One of the designers, Don Shepherd, stressed the importance of versatility in home office products: "We must take a good functional product and make it multifunctional," explaining that a desk could become an extension to a dining table, or a file cabinet could serve as an end table next to a sofa. Shepherd also stressed the importance of "rightness of size," explaining that most traditional office products are too big and too bulky for home offices. For his "Harvester" group of home office furniture, Shepherd and his partner, Tom Newhouse, wanted a directness in the design, inspired by Shaker furniture.

The Burdick Group's "workbench for executives" can be configured in a variety of ways, dividing paper-based tasks (in the components shown below) from storage and retrieval, computer and equipment use, communications, and a place to hold conferences.

Herman Miller for the Home
855 East Main Avenue
Zeeland, Michigan 49464
800-646-4400

Turnstone's ability to deliver and set-up office furniture at residential locations has been the hallmark of its home office line, which includes scaled-down or modified versions of Steelcase products.

Although high-end office furniture has been sold by regional distributors to medium and large businesses, Turnstone's approach is direct mail, offering substantial customer service by telephone. Turnstone offers desks, file cabinets, chairs, lamps, and other accessories.

A movable file unit, at left, stands next to a desking system featuring a retractable keyboard tray and a generous work surface in an L-shaped configuration. Lateral file storage and a supply cabinet are located to the right of the desk.

Turnstone Logistics

A subsidiary of the giant Steelcase, Turnstone provides furniture for home-based small businesses. Items in the Turnstone line appear similar to, if not the same as, other Steelcase products, but they are available in a more limited selection of finishes and colors and at substantially lower cost. Steelcase-Turnstone is able to charge less because it has eliminated dealers, decorators, and other resellers from its primary distribution channel, passing the savings on to the consumer.

The Turnstone solution combines traditional office desks, chairs, and storage units in a unique sales, delivery, and service environment tailored to small office/home office markets. Furthermore, Turnstone outsources direct mail marketing, teleservices, home delivery, and installation to a group it identifies as "virtual partners."

The problem of delivery and installation can be insurmountable for home office workers. Common carrier truckers generally are not welcome in residential neighborhoods, and they usually deliver only to the curb in the absence of a loading dock. Alternatively, parcel services do not deliver large furniture. Although moving companies do deliver to residences, they are seldom equipped or priced to make deliveries of one or two pieces to home offices.

To solve the problem, Steelcase went to NFC USA, a group of companies including Merchants Home Delivery, EXEL Logistics, and Allied Van Lines. NFC's strategic warehousing, delivery, and installation capabilities can reach nearly every home office in the country.

Turnstone's TS 315 line of chairs is designed for people whose work includes many different tasks involving sitting, reaching, swiveling, as well as getting up and moving around. The chairs combine a swivel-tilt feature with adjustable arms, and simple back, tension, and height adjustments.

Turnstone
A Steelcase Company
3528 Lousma Drive, SE
Wyoming, Michigan 49548
800-887-6789

Techline Planning and Design

Chul Park may have more experience designing home offices than anyone in the country. A Wisconsin-trained architect, Park manages a Techline gallery store in Rockville, Maryland, one of many outlets maintained by Marshall Erdman Associates, producers of the Techline system.

Planning a Techline home office is a pleasure for the customer, as Park rules out a measured grid and isometrically draws all of the system components freehand. This virtuoso performance combines his ability to select the right components for the space, use, and budget as each client presents a unique program of requirements. Techline components are mostly freestanding, combining custom-cut tops with a system of base units for file and drawer storage, open shelving, and wall-mounted shelving and cabinets. Techline manufactures companion units for other residential uses (television and stereo cabinets, beds, wardrobes, kitchen cabinets, etc.), all in a limited choice of laminate colors.

A Techline home office provides a built-in look from freestanding units, maximizing storage and surface areas. Where planning services are available, Techline provides extraordinary experience in developing small office and home office solutions that are straightforward and businesslike. Their services are particularly appropriate for installations that are separate from living areas, for apartment installations where space is limited, and for situations where the introduction of contemporary furniture design is appropriate.

With Techline components, it is difficult to see the difference between what is freestanding furniture and what is
built-in cabinetry. Indeed, none of the Techline system is in
fact built-in but is simply designed to look that way. The
cabinets, *opposite*, are complete boxes with backs and sides,
and are simply wall-hung with molly bolts. The desk surface,
above, and shelf above it are freestanding but are custom-
cut to fit the space exactly. A schematic of one of the infinite variety of Techline component configurations, *right*.

Techline
Marshall Erdman & Associates
5117 University Avenue
Madison, Wisconsin 53705
608-238-0211

Techline achieves a built-in look by deftly combining stock items with custom tops; clients can opt for professional installation services. Techline offices can be expanded, changed, or moved. The company also manufactures complementing components for kitchens, for stereo and televison systems, and for bedrooms, so that a Techline home office may be integrated into multipurpose spaces.

A black and cherry home office was designed by Techline for a narrow second-story landing, *opposite*. Custom shapes, as well as custom sizes, are also available for Techline work surfaces, *above right*. For home offices with uncommonly large storage requirements, yet another Techline system, such as the one *below*, may be the ideal solution.

Sligh Furniture Company's modular wall units make efficient use of vertical space; they often also have pathways between and behind to manage wires and cables. The unit *above*, combines a peninsula desk unit with open storage. Decorative corner connectors tie the units together.

A roll-top desk, *opposite*, is part of the Sligh Homestead Collection.

Human Factors at Sligh

Sligh Furniture Company is a 113-year-old family-owned company that specializes in desks and grandfather clocks. Jack Kelley, a Sligh designer formerly with Herman Miller, set out to discover home office preferences among 300 home office furniture buyers and their furniture dealers. Sligh first created desks for home use in 1934, but with the spread of microcomputers into residential settings, the market for home office furniture has changed. Sligh found that home workers ranked the issue of ample space for spreading out work as the most important feature in selecting home office furniture, with the need for plenty of knee space beneath the work area as equally important. Among the least important was furniture that concealed equipment and work when not in use. Kelley found that a majority of those responding to his survey wanted traditional or non-officelike furniture that could blend in unobtrusively and had a residential appearance.

After determining the number of work-at-home hours; the proportion of time spent working at the computer, talking on the phone, writing, reading, etc.; where work was accomplished; and the equipment used, respondents were asked what was important regarding their home office furniture. You may attempt to answer these questions before shopping for home office furniture. Using Kelley's checklist, rate each item as very important, somewhat important, or not important.

Appearance:
- Residential, comfortable appearance
- Modern, high-tech appearance
- Professional, high-quality appearance
- Blends with other furniture in the house/room

Arrangement:
- Ample surface for spreading out work
- More than one work surface
- Conceals work when not in use
- Keeps wires neat and out of the way

Space:
- Has plenty of space for books
- Has plenty of file space
- Has plenty of tackboards/marker boards
- Has plenty of space for displaying things

Quality and Features:
- Tough and durable
- Drawers are lockable
- Cabinets are lockable
- Comes completely assembled
- Storage for small things is easily rearrangeable
- Storage for large things is easily rearrangeable
- Fits in small space
- Is inexpensive
- Is an investment in quality

For Desk/Tables:
- Allows two people to work on it
- Is finished on all four sides
- Tablelike; knee room allows side-to-side mobility
- Knee-hole is deep and doesn't interfere with legs

For Computer-users:
- Is specifically designed to hold a computer
- Keeps nonessential computer components out of the way
- Conceals the computer when not in use
- Has a keyboard drawer/tray
- Decreases printer noise

Responsive to its finding that most people wanted traditional or non-officelike furniture, **Sligh** has designed a functional **Computer-Cabinet** with bifold doors, a folding **Pocket Chair**, a pull-out printer drawer on left, and a file drawer on right.

Sligh Furniture Company
1201 Industrial Avenue
Holland, Michigan 49423
616-392-7101

Sligh Furniture Company surveyed the home office furniture preferences of 300 home office furniture buyers and their furniture dealers.

Sligh's approach is to present 18th-century form to support contemporary functionality. Its Home Office Group includes the Correre Group, *above*, with stackable bookcase units, file units, door units (as shown at right of desk), and mobile file unit and deck over a corner desk (as shown left of desk).

A Homegrown Furniture Resource

Home/Suite/Office···2000®

In a category of its own is the Home/Suite/Office···2000, a system furniture collection developed by an interior designer. Joan Eisen of Livingston, New Jersey, is perhaps the first design practitioner to independently design and manufacture a line of home office furniture. Ms. Eisen's research validated what she had observed in her work for clients, that "the traditional office has become outdated," and that the consumer was having difficulty finding versatile and functional office furniture scaled to the home environment.

The Home/Suite/Office···2000 features overhead storage, concealed wire management, built-in task lighting, multiple configurations and four finishes. The system features a pull out pedestal for printer access and laminated tops for heavy duty use.

Joan Eisen Interiors
6 Aspen Drive
Livingston, New Jersey 07039
201-994-9510

DIRECTORY OF PRODUCTS & SERVICES

The needs of home office and small office workers have transformed the office equipment, office furniture, and accessories industries, forcing hundreds, indeed thousands of vendors to downsize their products and invent new ones, create new services, and find new channels for marketing and distribution.

Driving much of this re-engineering and downsizing has been the extraordinary advances in technology, particularly in telecommunications and computing, creating a seamless connection between corporations and their telecommuting workers communicating from their satellite home offices. These advances have also spawned a whole new category of small business that can operate as a virtual corporation, creating networks of workers across the country and around the world who communicate with each other and with their clients and customers using sophisticated voice and data services.

Office suppliers are continually challenged to keep up with rapidly changing ways of doing business, transforming technologies, and ever-tightening budgets.

This directory is a sampling of many of the new products and services available for the home office. While specific products or services listed here may have been eclipsed by new offerings, the directory provides the names and addresses of many of those companies focused on the home office market who are providing a continual stream of new ideas for their customers.

Many of the products and services listed here are available from office supply and computer retailers rather than directly from manufacturers. The addresses and phone numbers listed may be helpful in locating a retailer near you that carries a particular item.

Phoenix Designs, a wholly owned subsidiary of Herman Miller, Inc., has introduced a line of furniture for home offices and small offices that features quick delivery, simplicity, and affordability. The ergonomic Avian office chair, *opposite*, is a recent entry to the Phoenix line.

Bookcases

Book Box Library

Tower Bookcase

The Book Box from Levenger is 29¾ inches high by 29¾ inches wide, and either 9 or 15 inches deep. A single Book Box is credenza height, a stack of three stands 7½ feet tall. Each side of a Book Box has 21 shelf positions. The shelves slide over movable wire brackets. Optional doors are available, as are bases that lift the bottom ¾ inch off the floor.

Levenger's Tower Bookcase is 72 inches tall, ten inches deep, and sixteen inches wide. It comes with one fixed and five adjustable shelves. Made of Danish wood veneer in natural cherry, dark cherry, and medium oak.

Levenger
Tools for Serious Readers
975 South Congress Avenue
Delray Beach, FL 33445-4628
407-276-2436

Chairs

North Coast Medical, Inc.
187 Stauffer Boulevard
San Jose, CA 95125-1042
408-283-1900

The Patriot line of ergonomic office chairs from North Coast Medical has individualized arm, back, height, tension, and angle adjustments to correctly align and support all body types. The Patriot Executive Chair is a high-back chair with a seat height that adjusts from 17 to 22 inches.

**North Coast Medical Patriot
Executive Chair**

The Patriot Office Chair has the same adjustments as the Executive Chair, in a mid-back style. All Patriot Chairs have a five-year warranty and meet OSHA health and safety standards.

**North Coast Medical Patriot
Office Chair**

Herman Miller for the Home
855 East Main Avenue
Zeeland, MI 49464-9988
800-646-4400

The Equa Chair from Herman Miller is available in a wide range of options. It was named by *Time* magazine as among the "best designs of the decade" in 1990.

Equa Chair

Turnstone
3528 Lousma Drive SE
Wyoming, MI 49548-2251
616-246-1858

Turnstone's TS 315 line of chairs is designed for people who work at many different tasks involving sitting, reaching, swiveling, and getting up and moving around. The chairs combine a swivel-tilt feature with adjustable arms, and simple back, tension, and height adjustments.

TS 315 Chair

Computer Accessories

Chapter 4 of this book discusses some of the considerations involved in choosing computer equipment for a home office. The basic question of whether to buy a Macintosh or an IBM-compatible system is discussed, as are the criteria involved in selecting any piece of electronic equipment—features and capacities, user interface, space requirements, and other factors. The products shown here are only a few examples of state-of-the-art computer hardware available to the home office worker. If you wish to learn about all the different makes and models on the market today, consult one of the major magazines for the Macintosh world (e.g., *MacUser, MacWorld*) or the IBM-compatible field (e.g., *PC Week*). These magazines contain useful comparative product reviews and, generally, extensive buyers' guides.

Apple adjustable keyboard

Apple Computer's Adjustable Keyboard for Macintosh is a full-function keyboard whose left- and right-hand sections can be split to any angle up to thirty degrees. A separate extended numeric keypad has function keys and cursor-control keys. Both keyboard and keypad have adjustable feet for adjusting slope.

Apple Computer, Inc.
20525 Marani Avenue
Cupertino, CA 95014
408-996-1010

Turnstone Adjustable Keyboard Shelf

Turnstone's compact keyboard shelf is height-adjustable from work surface area to six inches below. It swivels 180 degrees, tilts fifteen degrees forward and fifteen degrees backward, stores under the work surface, and includes an adjustable palm rest.

Turnstone
3528 Lousma Drive SE
Wyoming, MI 49548-2251
616-246-1858

Scooter stand

Herman Miller's Scooter Stand is a freestanding, easily movable keyboard tray. It also functions as a writing table, slide projector platform, telephone stand, reference book holder, and lunch tray, among other things.

Herman Miller for the Home
855 East Main Avenue
Zeeland, MI 49464-9988
800-646-4400

Computer Hardware

Apple Computer, Inc.
20525 Marani Avenue
Cupertino, CA 95014
408-996-1010

If you're a nomadic sort who works on the road, at a weekend cottage, or at different places around your house, you'll probably want or need to check out laptop computers. There are many makes and models of IBM-compatible laptops; "Powerbooks" are Apple Computer's line. The 540C is Apple's top-of-the-line model. It has a 9.5-inch (diagonal) color screen. The computer is configured with a 320 mb hard disk, which can be replaced with a larger one.

Powerbook 540C

Apple Computer's Macintosh Performa 630 is described by the company as a "modular, multimedia computer for the home, education, and business." The Performa 630 and the other Macintosh models can be expanded and customized for various uses, including office workstation, video, and multimedia applications. The machine comes bundled with a variety of educational, reference, graphic, and multimedia software programs.

Mac Performa 630

Practical Peripherals
375 Conejo Ridge Avenue
Thousand Oaks, CA 91361
805-497-4774

A modem is a necessity if you want to use online systems, receive e-mail, or transmit electronic files to people at other locations. Practical Peripherals' PM288PKT VFC modem is a miniature pocket modem that fits into the palm of one's hand. Its data communication speed is 28,800 bps, and it has two RJ-11 ports, so that you can use your telephone without unplugging the modem.

PM288PKT VFC Pocket Modem

Copiers

In no other category of office equipment is the difference between large office machines and home office machines more dramatic than in the category of copiers. Desktop or "personal" copiers have fewer features, lower capacities, and slower speeds than the big machines. They are also far less expensive, and can save you many hours of precious time: most of your trips to the local copy center can be eliminated.

Canon PC850 Personal Copier

The Canon PC850 Personal Copier is a high-end machine that incorporates many of the capabilities and features included on Canon's business office copiers. The machine produces 16 copies per minute at letter size and prints up to 11-by-17-inch ledger copies. The zoom function reduces or enlarges originals in 1percent increments, from 49 to 204 percent of the size of the original.

Canon USA, Inc.
Home Office Products Division
One Canon Plaza
Lake Success, NY 11042
516-328-5145

Canon PC11RE Personal Copier

Another in Canon's PC Copiers line is the PC11RE. It copies documents at 10 copies per minute at sizes ranging from 2-by-3 ½-inch business cards to 8½-by-14-inch legal size paper. The copier's replaceable Single Cartridge System contains everything that can run-out or wear-out, including the drum, development unit, and toner.

Mita Copystar America, Inc.
225 Sand Road
P.O. Box 40008
Fairfield, NJ 07004-0008
201-808-8444

The Mita DC-1755 is a "low-volume" desktop copier that produces 17 copies per minute. One feature enables the user to produce professional quality overhead transparencies. The machine's positively charged ruby drum reduces the amount of ozone the copier would otherwise generate.

Mita DC-1755 copier

Sharp Electronics Corporation
Sharp Plaza
Mahwah, NJ 07430-2135
201-529-8200

The Sharp Z-20 copier makes three copies per minute and warms up in less than twenty seconds. It weighs 14.8 pounds and takes up less than 1.4 square feet of surface space.

Sharp Z-20 copier

Xerox Corporation
Personal Document Products
Division
300 Main Street, Suite 20
East Rochester, NY 14454
203-968-3000

The Xerox 5201 personal copier makes three letter-size copies per minute. It warms up in five seconds and weighs fourteen pounds. The copier has a handle for carrying.

Xerox 5201 personal copier

The 5222 personal copier produces five copies per minute. The machine copies both letter and legal size paper, and its paper tray holds forty sheets. The 5222 is customer-installable and weighs approximately 24 pounds.

Xerox 5222 personal copier

Desks & Tables

Today's home office worker can choose from a large array of furniture products designed specifically for home offices. You probably will not have difficulty in finding individual pieces, or coordinated sets, of furniture that fit your use requirements (e.g., standing vs. sitting; stationary vs. moving around) and that create the image you want to project for your home office. In addition, all the leading office furniture manufacturers today are sensitive to two requirements of most home office workers: the need for office furniture to be harmonious with the furnishings and decor of the rest of the house; and the need to use ergonomically sound desks and surfaces, workstations, chairs, lighting, and equipment.

Desk from the TD Collection

This table desk from the TD Collection was specifically designed for people who work at home. The collection includes table desks, storage cabinets, bookcases, work organizers, and other components.

Herman Miller for the Home
855 East Main Avenue
Zeeland, MI 49464-9988
800-646-4400

Computer Group

Levenger's three-piece Computer Group has a pull-out keyboard tray, a Cooper's Cabinet on the left, and a three-drawer cabinet on the right. The top is an inch-thick piece of solid cherry or oak. Stainless steel levelers are hidden under the side panels.

Levenger
Tools for Serious Readers
975 South Congress Avenue
Delray Beach, FL 33445-4628
407-276-2436

MicroComputer
Accessories, Inc.
9920 La Cienega Boulevard
P.O. Box 17032
Inglewood, CA 90308-7032
310-645-9400

The SnapEase Computer Desk and Hutch from MicroComputer Accessories, Inc., assemble without tools. The Computer Desk features a unique full-width glide-out keyboard drawer. The desk is 46 inches wide, 28 inches deep, and 30 inches high. Both units are available in black or eggshell white and feature a durable, scratch-resistant construction.

SnapEase Ready-to-Assemble Furniture

Turnstone
P.O. Box 1967
Grand Rapids, MI 49316
616-698-4487

The Turnstone TS 520 is an L-shaped desk that features integrated cable management. Complementing the desk is a TS 315 multifunction, ergonomically adjustable chair and a mobile file that rolls under the desk.

TS 520 desking

Versteel
P.O. Box 850
Jasper, IN 47547-0850
800-876-2120

This 42-inch diameter round table from Versteel is height-adjustable from typing level (26¾ inches) to wheelchair height (33 inches). Tables are available with optional removable top, tilt-top, or casters.

42-inch round table

Ergonomic Accessories

North Coast Medical WristAir

The WristAir Pad from North Coast Medical is designed to help protect the wrist against cumulative trauma injuries by supporting it in the optimal position for using a mouse. The wrist pad is one inch thick.

North Coast Medical, Inc.
187 Stauffer Boulevard
San Jose, CA 95125-1042
408-283-1900

North Coast Medical CRT Valet

North Coast Medical's CRT Valet is an ergonomically designed mount for your computer monitor. Its adjustable arm extends, retracts, and rotates, holding the monitor on a tilt and swivel base for correct viewing position. The unit can be mounted to a flat surface or a wall.

North Coast Medical WordySturdy

North Coast Medical's WordySturdy copy holder supports multiple documents and manuals. It can be switched to either side of the computer screen without disassembling, and can also be used freestanding on the desktop.

North Coast Medical, Inc.
187 Stauffer Boulevard
San Jose, CA 95125-1042
408-283-1900

The Geneva Task Light provides controllable diffused lighting for individual workstations. Each of the three joints connecting the two arms and the light head have multiple adjustments, and the light head swivels 120 degrees and tilts 180 degrees. A single-arm style is also available. The products carry a five-year manufacturer's warranty.

North Coast Medical Geneva Task Light

The WorkMod Footrest has multiple positions adjustable by the slightest pressure from the feet. The apparatus even moves with your feet when stretching your legs.

North Coast Medical WorkMod Footrest

Turnstone
3528 Lousma Drive, SE
Wyoming, MI 49548-2251
616-246-1858

Turnstone's vinyl-clad footrest supports the user's legs and improves circulation by raising the feet two to six inches above the floor. The angle can be changed merely by shifting your feet.

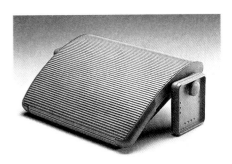

Turnstone Footrest

Fax Machines

Canon Faxphone B160

The Faxphone B160 from Canon's Home Office Products Division operates as a stand-alone fax or as a printer. The B160 is the company's first integrated multifunction home office product that uses a parallel interface for connection to a personal computer. This connection allows the user to operate the B160 as a printer.

Canon USA, Inc.
Home Office Products Division
One Canon Plaza
Lake Success, NY 11042
516-328-5145

FX5500 Plain Paper Fax

Samsung's FX5500 Plain Paper Fax is a multifunctional machine, serving as a telephone, copy machine, fax, and answering machine. It has a nine-second transmission speed, a 20-sheet automatic document feeder, and can store 20 one-touch programmable numbers and fifty two-touch programmable numbers.

Samsung Electronics America, Inc.
105 Challenger Road
Ridgefield, NJ 07660
201-229-4000

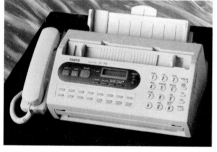

SFX-P50 Fax

Sanyo's SFX-P50 is a compact desktop inkjet plain paper fax machine. It has a capacity of 100 sheets and a transmission time of approximately 24 seconds in fine mode, 12 seconds in standard mode, and 9 seconds in standard (MMR) mode.

Sanyo Fisher Corporation USA
21350 Lassen Street
Chatsworth, CA 91311
818-998-7322

UX-184 Facsimile

The UX-184 fax machine from Sharp features fax/phone changeover, a ten-page auto document feeder, and an automatic paper cutter. A built-in timer allows the user to take advantage of favorable after-hours telephone rates. An autodial function allows the user to store and access up to 50 frequently dialed numbers.

Sharp Electronics Corporation
Sharp Plaza
Mahwah, NJ 07430-2135
201-529-8200

Fax/Modem Products & Services

No matter what type of business you conduct at your home office, sooner or later you will need to send or receive electronic information instantaneously. When you do, you'll be using an on-line information service. Going on-line may be a relatively simple matter, such as sending or receiving e-mail; or accessing financial or consumer information on a commercial on-line service such as Dow Jones Information Retrieval or Prodigy; or exploring the huge information mega-network, /the Internet.

America Online
8619 Westwood Center Drive
Vienna, VA 22182-2285
703-448-8700

America Online (AOL) is an on-line service offering a number of popular magazines, as well as a variety of other information. AOL has as graphical user interface and provides a connection to the Internet.

America Online

CompuServe
P.O. Box 20212
5000 Arlington Centre Blvd.
Columbus, OH 43220
614-457-8600

CompuServe Information Service is a general-interest on-line system that offers a basic service for a monthly fee and hourly charges for premium services. The basic service includes e-mail, news, sports, reference publications, shopping, financial data, travel, entertainment, and games. Special interest forums allow you to share ideas with people around the world.

Hello Direct
5884 Eden Park Place
San Jose, CA 95138-1859
800-444-3556

The Vomax voice and fax mail system forwards both voice and fax messages to designated phone numbers or fax machines. Containing a full megabyte of memory, the Vomax can store a combination of thirty pages of fax messages or twenty minutes of phone messages. Fax/modem software and a 14,400 bps modem are included.

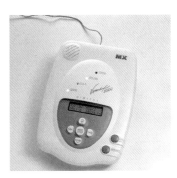

Vomax

Office Accessories & Supplies

Many home workers design their home offices after a long stint working in the offices of a medium- or large-sized corporation, finding that the home versions of computers, printers, copiers, typewriters, phones and faxes are much different from their corporate counterparts. Your printer is likely to be smaller, slower, and have less memory. Your copier will probably be a trimmed-down version of the workhorse that churned out a thousand copies a day at your old company. Your computer may be the one major machine that stays the same in the transition, but it probably won't be hooked up to an elaborate multiuser network. The products shown and described below are a sampling of current product offerings of office accessories specifically designed for home offices.

Deluxe Phone Stand

The Deluxe Phone Stand from Hello Direct creates a storage area under your telephone for message pads, phone book, or other material you want at the ready. The stand is constructed of clear acrylic and supports eight pounds.

Hello Direct
5884 Eden Park Place
San Jose, CA 95138-1859
800-444-3556

Telescoping Telephone Arm

Hello Direct's Telescoping Telephone Arm moves your phone up or down, closer or further away. The post rotates 360 degrees and locks in place as you desire, and the phone platform swivels.

Levenger
Tools for Serious Readers
975 South Congress Avenue
Delray Beach, FL 33445-4628
407-276-2436

Levenger's Footrest rocks easily back and forth and takes pressure off the undersides of your legs and lower back. Made of solid ash inlaid with rubber tile.

Footrest

Levenger's Oak Magazine Box is made from ¾-inch solid oak with finger joints on four sides, and has a solid brass pull. The box holds 3½ inches of magazines.

Wood Magazine Box

The Desk Organizer from Levenger is made from solid cherry or oak. The compartments are designed to hold diskettes, letter-size paper, and business envelopes. The piece measures 36½ inches long, 12½ inches wide, and 16 inches high.

Desk Organizer

Levenger makes several Project Boxes of Danish wood veneer in natural cherry, dark cherry, and medium oak. The boxes range from 4 to 14 compartments. Drawers (in pairs) are available and fit any compartment.

Project Box

Paper Access catalog

The Paper Access catalog offers recycled, business, and specialty papers, and accessories and presentation materials.

Paper Access
23 West 18th Street
New York, NY 10011
800-727-3701

PaperKit

The PaperKit from PaperDirect contains more than100 ready-to-use 8½-by-11-inch papers in different styles, colors, and weights, as well as some envelopes. Both the PaperKit and the PaperSelector, a swatch kit (not shown), are free with a minimum order from the PaperDirect Paper Catalog, which offers a variety of papers and accessories.

PaperDirect, Inc.
P.O. Box 677
205 Chubb Avenue
Lyndhurst, NJ 07071-0677
800-272-7377

Full Sheet Disk Holder

The Full Sheet Disk Holder from PaperDirect is a 3-hole-punched plastic sleeve that holds a diskette and 8½-by-11-inch paper. Packaged in boxes of ten holders.

PaperDirect, Inc.
P.O. Box 677
205 Chubb Avenue
Lyndhurst, NJ 07071-0677
800-272-7377

The Five-Drawer Paper Storage
Cabinet from PaperDirect has molded, easily opened drawers. The bottom drawer holds a ream of paper.

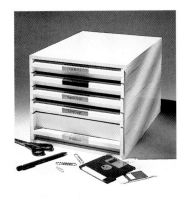

5-Drawer Storage Cabinet

"Presentation to Go," from
PaperDirect, is a 9-by-12-inch binder
that folds open and stands up as an
easel. It contains 10 clear plastic
pouches and has a carrying handle.

Presentation to Go

Sanyo Fisher Corporation USA
21350 Lassen Street
Chatsworth, CA 91311
818-998-7322

Sanyo's SBS-620 paper shredder slits
up to nine sheets of paper at a time at
17 feet per minute into approximately
⅛-inch-wide strips. Features include
self-sharpening steel cutters, a sensor
switch that automatically starts and
stops operation, and a reverse function
for unjamming paper.

Paper Shredder

Phones & Answering Machines

Speakerphone 1545

AT&T's Digital Answering System Speakerphone 1545 allows up to 26 minutes of recording time for the outgoing announcement and incoming messages. The system features a voice mailbox which gives users the ability to record messages in four different "mailboxes" and present more than one announcement to callers.

AT&T
5 Wood Hollow Road
Parsipany, NJ 07054
212-841-4666

HelloSet Ultralight

The HelloSet Cordless telephone headset from HelloDirect weighs seven ounces, has a rotatable microphone boom arm, and works up to 50 feet away from the phone base. The headset uses a 900 MHz frequency, with a 32-channel capacity. The headset works on all types of business phones.

Hello Direct
5884 Eden Park Place
San Jose, CA 95138-1859
800-444-3556

AT&T 2-line Remote Answering Machine

The Hello Direct catalog offers this AT&T two-line remote answering machine. The dual microcassette system answers calls on both lines. Other features include voice help menu, selective playback, call intercept, toll saver, and a play-new-messages-only option.

AT&T Cordless Intercom/Speakerphone

The Hello Direct catalog offers the AT&T Cordless Intercom/Speakerphone which features a handset and base, both with built-in dialpads. The base has a speakerphone, so calls can be made from either unit. The phone can be taken up to 1,000 feet from the base in ideal conditions and automatically selects the clearest of ten channels before you lift the handset.

Hello Direct
5884 Eden Park Place
San Jose, CA 95138-1859
800-444-3556

The Tropez Digital Headset Phone from Hello Direct combines a headset and cordless phone in a single product. The headset plugs into the cordless handset, and the handset is carried in a special leather "glove" that clips to your belt. Three different headset styles are available.

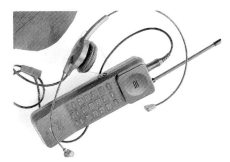

Tropez Digital Headset Phone

Motorola Communications
Cellular Subscriber Group
1475 West Shure Drive
Arlington Heights, IL 60004

Motorola's MicroTAC Elite is a cellular phone that weighs just 3.9 ounces. Its lithium ion batteries offer up to sixty minutes of talk time or ten hours of standby time. An optional digital answering machine answers in your own voice so callers can leave a short voice message. An optional pager feature is also available.

MicroTAC Cellular Telephone

Motorola Communications
1303 East Algonquin Road
Schaumburg, IL 60196
708-576-5000

The Memo Express Alpha Pager from Motorola provides the audible alert of a beeper and displays the phone number as a numeric pager does; but it also receives and displays word messages. The Memo Express stores up to 15 messages, which may be up to 120 characters long.

Memo Express Alpha Pagers

Sharp Electronics Corporation
Sharp Plaza
Mahwah, NJ 07430-2135
201-529-8200

The CL-300(W) Cordless Telephone from Sharp Electronics Corporation features an illuminated keypad and a ten-channel auto select feature which prevents interference with other cordless phones within a 100-meter range. The phone has twenty one-touch auto dial numbers and a long-life battery that operates for at least 21 days after being charged.

CL-300(W) Cordless Telephone

Portable Office Equipment

Canon Calculator P120-DH

Among the many useful desktop calculators on the market is the Canon P120-DH. Aimed at the home office and small business user, this medium-to heavy-duty usage machine features a large, 12-digit liquid crystal display (LCD) and two-color high speed ink roller with the printing performance of an ink ribbon machine.

Canon USA, Inc.
Home Office Products
Division
One Canon Plaza
Lake Success, NY 11042
516-328-5145

Olivetti DM-118 Electronic Organizer

The Royal DM118 from Olivetti Office USA is a simple and inexpensive electronic organizer with 18K memory. It can store 700 items such as names, addresses, and telephone and fax numbers.

Olivetti Office USA
765 U.S. Highway 202
Bridgewater, NJ 09907-0945
908-526-8200

Sanyo TRC 660M MicroCassette Recorder

One of the many good-quality microcassette recorders is the Sanyo TRC 660M, including standard features such as one-touch record, pause, 3-digit tape counter, built-in microphone, and external jack. It also has a voice-activated recording system.

Sanyo Fisher Corporation USA
21350 Lassen Street
Chatsworth, CA 91311
818-998-7322

Seiko Instruments USA, Inc.
Consumer Products Division
2990 West Lomita Boulevard
Torrance, CA 90505
310-517-7700

Seiko Instruments USA offers a line of portable electronic translators incorporating the Berlitz database of words and phrases. The TR2201 Spanish/English translator has more than 300 categorized phrases and 40,000 translations, and a 31-character scrolling dot-matrix display.

Seiko Berlitz Spanish/English translator TR2201

Another portable electronic accessory from Seiko is the WP-1101 spell checker. A related product is the WP-1201 electronic thesaurus, which can retrieve more than 80,000 words or 500,000 synonyms.

Seiko Electronic spell checker

Sharp Electronics Corporation
Sharp Plaza
Mahwah, NJ 07430-2135
201-529-8200

The OZ-9500 Wizard electronic organizer from Sharp Electronics Corporation features a graphical user interface with icon buttons, pull-down menus, and copy and paste capabilities. It combines a touch-screen LCD, pen input technology, an integrated filing system, and wireless infrared communications. The model shown at *right* is coupled with an optional fax/modem (model CE-FM4) and adapter (model CE-137T).

Sharp OZ-9500 Wizard electronic organizer

Printers

The category of laser printers for home offices has arrived at a happy state. Printers with 300 dpi resolution and even 600 dpi (and, in one case, 720 dpi) are now becoming affordable for many workers. And the leading manufacturers, Hewlett-Packard and Apple Computer, have models for both IBM-compatible PC and Macintosh systems.

LaserWriter Select 360

Apple Computer's LaserWriter Select 360 is designed for use in both Mac and combined Mac/Windows environments. It has a 600-dpi resolution and prints at 10 pages per minute. The company also manufactures the less expensive Personal LaserWriter 320, a 300-dpi printer that prints four pages per minute and includes Adobe PostScript Level 2.

Apple Computer, Inc.
20525 Marani Avenue
Cupertino, CA 95014
408-996-1010

Epson Stylus printer

The Epson Stylus color ink jet printer has both a 360-dpi resolution mode and also a "superfine" mode that prints at a resolution of 720-dpi on coated paper. The printer is available for both IBM-compatible environments (Windows and DOS) and Macintosh.

Epson America
20770 Madrona Avenue
Torrance, CA 90503
310-782-0770

Hewlett-Packard
19310 Pruneridge Avenue
Cupertino, CA 95014
415-857-4819

The Hewlett-Packard LaserJet 4L printer is the company's lowest-priced personal laser printer. It prints at four pages per minute at a resolution of 300 dpi and includes Memory Enhancement technology, which effectively doubles standard memory. The company also makes the LaserJet 4LM printer, which works with the Macintosh.

H-P LaserJet 4L printer

Seiko Instruments USA, Inc.
Compact Convenience
Peripherals Division
1130 Ringwood Court
San Jose, CA 95131
408-922-5800

Seiko's Smart Label Printer Plus, for IBM-compatible computers, is an electronic way to address envelopes and make labels. Usable with either Windows- or DOS-based PCs, the device includes both hardware and software. The unit, which uses thermal printer technology, weighs one pound. The Smart Label line also includes a more advanced machine, the Smart Label Printer Pro.

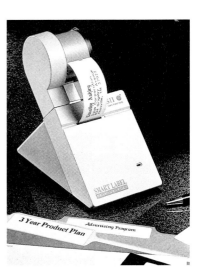

Seiko Smart Label Printer Plus

Publications

An increasing number of home office worker are self-employed, many for the first time. There are a number of books, periodicals, and newsletters directed at home office-based entrepreneurs and small business owners. Other publications are directed more generally to all home office workers, including telecommuters.

Entrepreneur **monthly magazine**

Entrepreneur is a monthly magazine for small- and medium-size businesses. Monthly departments cover finance, taxation, marketing, trends, travel, the Small Business Administration, and other topics important to home office workers. Each issue has feature articles, often on the strategies and tactics used by a single company or a selected group of companies to solve problems that commonly confront small and growing businesses.

Entrepreneur Magazine
2392 Morse Avenue
Irvine, CA 92714

Home Office Computing
monthly magazine

Home Office Computing is a monthly magazine on the uses of personal computers by home office workers and entrepreneurs. Monthly feature articles focus on the experiences of individuals, discuss trends, and present results of reader surveys. Monthly product reviews cover current and popular hardware and software used in home offices.

Home Office Computing
411 Lafayette Street
4th Floor
New York, NY 10003
212-505-4220

Office Depot
Home Business Advisor
2200 Old Germantown Road
Delray Beach, FL   33445

Office Depot Home Business Advisor is a quarterly newsletter published by Office Depot, Inc., an office supply company. The publication features articles and sidebars on topics such as marketing, finance, networking, home office habits, and psychology.

**Office Depot
Home Business Advisor**

Telecommuting Review:
The Gordon Report
10 Donner Court
Monmouth Junction, NJ
08852
908-329-2266

For every niche, it seems, there's a newsletter. The home office niche—a pretty large one today—has its share of newsletters. *Telecommuting Review: The Gordon Report* is a monthly newsletter with articles on products, services, problems, and trends of interest to work-at-home telecommuters. The newsletter also reports study findings and announces events such as conferences and seminars.

Typewriters

Canon StarWriter Pro 5000 Personal Publishing System

Canon StarWriter 400 Personal Publishing System

The Canon StarWriter Pro 5000 Personal Publishing System has two components: a keyboard/printer unit, which prints at a 360-dpi resolution, and a 14-inch CRT monitor with 16 shades of gray. The keyboard/printer unit contains a 3.5-inch, 1.44 mb disk drive. Diskettes included with the system contain proprietary clip art software and illustrations.

Canon's StarWriter 400 Personal Publishing System prints documents at 360-dpi resolution, and can print 325 different characters plus 212 scientific and graphic symbols. The machine contains 28KB internal text memory and a 3.5-inch disk drive. The keyboard, LCD display, printer, and disk drive are all contained in the unit.

Canon USA, Inc.
Home Office Products Division
One Canon Plaza
Lake Success, NY 11042
516-328-5145

Workstations

Davis Furniture
Industries, Inc.
2401 South College Drive
P.O. Box 2065
High Point, NC 27261-2065
910-889-2009

The TAO collection from Davis Furniture Industries (under a license from the German firm Wilhelm Renz & Company) is a modular series of desks, workstations, pedestals, and conference tables that can be combined in a variety of configurations. Accessory tops are attached to the stationary desk top in a way that allows the tops to rotate or "float" over the desk top. Legs can be adjusted to provide for different levels of table tops.

TAO Home Office #1

TAO Home Office #2

Ergotron
3450 Yankee Drive
Suite 100
Eagan, MN 55121-1627
612-452-8135

The Freestanding Workstation from Ergotron was designed to be positioned behind existing drafting and design tables. The unit includes a rear rail suspension shelf, monitor caddy, keyboard holder, and peripheral table.

Freestanding Workstation

Ergotron's Wall Mount Workstation is designed to mount computer equipment on office walls, factory pallet racking, or other sturdy vertical platforms. It can be used anywhere there is no space to place a workstation behind a drafting table or other work surface.

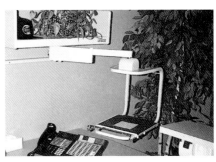

Wall Mount Workstation

215

Telephone Services

Your local telephone company or its regional affiliate offers a mix of basic and custom services. The custom calling features vary somewhat from place to place, but commonly include some or all of the following: answer call, call waiting, call return, caller ID, call forwarding, conference calling, call screening, and "portable," personal long distance numbers such as AT&T's 500 Service.

AT&T True Connections service is a personal long distance number where you may be reached wherever you are. You are assigned a 500 number that always stays the same. Then, as you roam around, you dial in a code on the phone where you're stopping or staying and the people to whom you've given your 500 number can reach you there. AT&T, of course, also offers a variety of long distance and custom calling services.

AT&T, MCI, and Sprint are the three major long distance companies in the United States. There are also smaller companies called long distance "brokers" or "packagers" that often offer discount rates. These companies include Allnet Communications, ExpressTel, and Telegration.

AT & T
1301 Avenue of the Americas
New York, NY 10019

MCI Communications
1801 Pennsylvania Avenue, NW
Washington, DC 20006
800-289-0073

Allnet Communications
30300 Telegraph Road
Bingham Farms, MI 48025
810-647-6920

Sprint
8140 Ward Parkway
Kansas City, MO 64114
913-624-6000

ExpressTel
324 South State Street, #125
Salt Lake City, UT 84111
800-748-4000

Telegration
12700 Fair Lakes Circle, #200
Fairfax, VA 22033
703-242-0640

CREDITS

2: Design by Joan Halperin. Photo copyright 1987 by Darwin K. Davidson, courtesy of Darwin K. Davidson and Joan Halperin/Interior Design **3:** Photo of Rosenbaum residence by Sergio Reyes. **5:** Design by Sam Davis. Photo by Christopher Irion, courtesy of Davis & Joyce Architects. **6:** *Top left:* Design by Michael B. Lehrer. Drawing courtesy of Lehrer Architects. *Top right:* Design by Thomas Tomsich, AIA. Drawing courtesy of Tomsich Associates, Architects/Planners/Interior Designers. *Bottom left:* Design by Elizabeth B. Gillin. Photo by Melabee M. Miller, courtesy of Elizabeth B. Gillin Interiors, ASID. *Bottom right:* TAO Home Office Collection from Davis Furniture Industries, Inc.. Photo courtesy of Davis Furniture Industries, Inc. **7:** *Top left:* Royal RFX 2100 plain paper fax machine. Photo by Don Eldridge Associates, courtesy of Olivetti Office USA. *Top right:* Burdick Group™ designed by Bruce Burdick for Herman Miller, Inc. Photo courtesy of Herman Miller, Inc. *Bottom left:* Design by Bradley Rytz. Photo by Sharon Risedorph, courtesy of Bradley Rytz. *Bottom right:* Levenger Desk Organizer Photo courtesy of Levenger "Tools for Serious Readers" Catalog Company. **8:** Design by Patricia Eichman. Photo courtesy of Patricia Eichman Interior Design. **9:** Photo of Rosenbaum residence by Sergio Reyes. **11:** Ethan Allen Office at Home, Georgian Court style.. Photo reproduced with permission of Ethan Allen Inc., the copyright holder. **12, 15:** Design by Carolin M. Schebish, ASID. Photo by Reyndell Stockman, courtesy of Design Exchange, Inc. **16–17:** Design by Joan Halperin. Photos copyright 1987 by Darwin K. Davidson, courtesy of Darwin K. Davidson and Joan Halperin/interior Design. **18–19:** Photo of Rosenbaum House, Florence, Alabama, courtesy of Mildred Rosenbaum. **20:** *Top:* Swagged Leg Group designed by George Nelson for Herman Miller, Inc. (1958–1964). *Middle:* Executive Office Group designed by Gilbert Rhode for Herman Miller, Inc. (1942–1948). *Bottom:* Action Office® Series 1 freestanding components, concept by Robert Propst designed by George Nelson for Herman Miller, Inc. (1964–1971). Photos courtesy of Herman Miller, Inc. **21:** Office-residential desk designed by George Nelson for Herman Miller, Inc. (1946–c. 1957). Photo courtesy of Herman Miller, Inc. **22–25:** Design by Michael B. Lehrer. Photos by Grant Mudford and Dominique Vorillion. Photos and drawing courtesy of Lehrer Architects. **26:** Home Office Group from Sligh Furniture Co. Photo courtesy of Sligh Furniture Co. **27:** Burdick Group designed by Bruce Burdick for Herman Miller, Inc. Photo by Bill Sharpe, courtesy of Herman Miller, Inc. **28:** Ethan Allen Office at Home, American Impressions style. Photo reproduced with permission of Ethan Allen Inc., the copyright holder. **30:** Eames® lounge and ottoman. Designed by Charles Eames for Herman Miller, Inc. Photo by Phil Schaafsma courtesy of Herman Miller, Inc. **31:** Burdick Group table designed by Bruce Burdick for Herman Miller, Inc. Photo by Bill Sharpe, courtesy of Herman Miller, Inc. **32:** Design by James C. Williams. Photo courtesy of James C. Williams, Architect. **34:** Eames® products pictured in the home office of Jack Lenor Larsen. Photo by Elliott Kaufman, courtesy of Herman Miller, Inc. **35:** Relay® furniture and Eames® products in the home office of Jack Lenor Larsen. Photo by Elliott Kaufman, courtesy of Herman Miller, Inc. **36:** Design by Thomas Tomsich, AIA. Drawing courtesy of Tomsich Associates, Architect/Planners/Interior Designers. **38–42:** Design by Thomas J. Quarticelli. Drawings and photos copyright Thomas J. Quarticelli 1994. **43:** Design by Freya Block. Photo by Scott Bowron, courtesy of Freya Block Design, Inc. **44–45:** Design by Alvin Schneider. Photos courtesy of Alvin Schneider Design. **47:** Design by Donald Eurich. Drawing by Donald Eurich, courtesy of Eurich & Associates. **48–49:** Design by Dale Naegle. Drawing and photos courtesy of Dale W. Naegle, FAIA. **51–53:** Design by Joan Ravasy. Photos courtesy of Joan Ravasy, ASID. **54–55, 56, 57:** Design by Ray Townsley (exteriors) and Bruce Williams (interiors). Photos courtesy of Ray Townsley. **58–63:** Photos of Rosenbaum residence by Sergio Reyes. **64, 67–69, 71:** Design by Elizabeth B. Gillin. Photos by Melabee M. Miller, courtesy of Elizabeth B. Gillin Interiors, ASID. **72, 74–77:** Design by Thomas Tomsich, AIA. Photos and drawing courtesy of Tomsich Associates, Architects/Planners/Interior Designers. **79–81:** Design by Davis & Joyce Architects. Photos copyright Christopher Irion. **82–83:** Design by Sally Groth. Photos courtesy of Dawn Kearney, Design Line Interiors, Inc. **84, 86:** Design by Freya Block. Photo by Freya Block, courtesy of Freya Block Design, Inc. **85, 89:** Design by Freya Block. Photo by Scott Bowron, courtesy of Freya Block Design, Inc. **90–92:** Design by Maria and Daniel Levin. Photo courtesy of CHIMERA (Interior Surface Arts). **94–95:** Design by William W. Stubbs, IIDA. Photo by Rob Muir, courtesy of William W. Stubbs, IIDA. **96:** Design by Ray Townsley. Photo courtesy of Ray Townsley. **97:** Design by Beverley Forster. Photo courtesy of Beverley Forster Interior Design, San Francisco. **98:** Ergon 2® chair designed by Bill Stumpf for Herman Miller, Inc. Photo by Bill Sharpe, courtesy of Herman Miller, Inc. **100:** Relay® furniture designed by Geoff Hollington for Herman Miller, Inc. Photo by Elliott Kaufman, courtesy of Herman Miller, Inc. **101:** Drawings by Jack Kelley. Courtesy of Sligh Furniture Co. **102–103:** TAO Home Office Collection from Davis Furniture Industries, Inc.. Photos courtesy of Davis Furniture Industries, Inc. **104:** Techline home office components. Photo courtesy of Techline: designed and manufactured by Marshall Erdman & Assoc. **105:** Ethan Allen wood desk. Photo reproduced with permission of Ethan Allen Inc., the copyright holder. **106:** Design by Mary Ann McEwan, ASID. Photos by Russell Abraham Photography, courtesy of Mary Ann McEwan, ASID. **107:** Techline home office components. Photo courtesy of Techline: designed and manufactured by Marshall Erdman & Assoc. **108:** Eames® lounge and ottoman designed by Charles Eames for Herman Miller, Inc. Photo by Earl Woods, courtesy of Herman Miller, Inc. **109:** *Top:* Eames® molded plywood chair designed by Charles Eames for Herman Miller, Inc. Photo by Phil Schaafsma, courtesy of Herman Miller, Inc. *Bottom left:* Ergon 2® footrest designed by Bill Stumpf for Herman Miller, Inc. Photo courtesy of Herman Miller, Inc. **Bottom right:** Bulldog Task Armchair from The Knoll Group. Photo by Bill White, courtesy of The Knoll Group. **110,** *top,* and **111:** Patriot Ergonomic Office Chairs from North Coast Medical, Inc. **110,** *bottom:* WorkMod Footrest from North Coast Medical, Inc.. Photos courtesy of North Coast Medical, Inc. **112:** Ergon 2® chair designed by Bill Stumpf for Herman Miller, Inc. Photo by Bill Sharpe, courtesy of Herman Miller, Inc. **113:** Surf Computer Accessories from The Knoll Group. Photo by David Riley, courtesy of The Knoll Group. **114:** Techline home office configuration. Drawing courtesy of Techline: designed and manufactured by Marshall Erdman & Assoc. **115:** Levenger Wood Magazine Box, Photo courtesy of Levenger "Tools for Serious Readers" Catalog Company. **116:** Techline home office components. Photo courtesy of Techline: designed and manufactured by Marshall Erdman & Assoc. **117:** Design by Shelli Oreck Photo by Marion Brenner, courtesy of Shelli Oreck **118:** Design by Gail Whiting. Photo courtesy of Gail Whiting Design Consultants. **119:** Levenger Project Box. **120,** *top:* Levenger Book Box Library. **120,** *bottom:* Levenger Desk Organizer. Photos courtesy of Levenger "Tools for Serious Readers" Catalog Company. **121,** *top:* Levenger Tower Bookcase. **121,** bottom: Levenger Computer Group. Photos courtesy of Levenger "Tools for Serious Readers Catalog Company. **122:** Design by Richard and Shelley Hall. Photo by Susan Seitz, courtesy of Richard L. Hall Enterprises. **123:** Design by Richard and Shelley Hall. Photo courtesy of Richard L. Hall Enterprises. **124:** Techline home office components. Photo courtesy of Techline:

designed and manufactured by MarshalI Erdrnsn & Assoc. **126**: Turnstone TS520 desk. Photo by Craig vanderLende, courtesy of Turnstone. **127, 130, 133, 135, 137**: Illustrations by Jennifer Cosgrove, courtesy of The Rosenbaum Group, Inc. **128**: WordySturdy from North Coast Medical, Inc. **129**: CRT Valet from North Coast Medical, Inc. Photos courtesy of North Coast Medical, Inc. **132**: Canon StarWriter 400 Personal Publishing System. Photo courtesy of Canon USA, Inc. **134**: TD Collection designed by Tom Newhouse and Don Shepherd for Herman Miller, Inc. Photograph by Elliott Kaufman, courtesy of Herman Miller, Inc. (Computer is an Apple Powerbook 540C.)**136**: HP LaserJet 4L Printer from Hewlett-Packard. Photo courtesy of Hewlett-Packard. **138**, *top*: SnapEase Ready-to-Assemble Furniture from Rubbermaid Office Products Inc. Photo courtesy of Rubbermaid Office Products Inc. **138**, *bottom*: WristAir Mouse Pad from North Coast Medical, Inc. Photo courtesy of North Coast Medical, Inc.**139, 144, 145**: Home Office products designed by Jean Beirise for Herman Miller, Inc. Photos by Roger Hill and drawing by Jean Beirise, courtesy of Herman Miller, Inc. **140**: Royal RFX 2100 plain paper fax machine. Photo by Don Eldridge Associates, courtesy of Olivetti Office USA. **142**: Canon PC11RE Personal Copier. **143**: Canon Faxphone 17A. Photos courtesy of Canon USA Inc. **146**: Deluxe Phone Stand. **147**: AT&T Cordless Intercom/Speakerphone. **148**: AT&T 2-Line Remote Answering Machine. **149**: AT&T Digital Answering System Speakerphone. **150**: Tropez Digital Headset Phone. All available from Hello Direct Catalog of Telephone Productivity Tools. Photos courtesy of Hello Direct Catalog of Telephone Productivity Tools. **151**: Reprint permission granted by AOL. All rights reserved. **152**: Design Workcenter from Ergotron. Photo courtesy of Ergotron, Inc. **154**: Burdick Group designed by Bruce Burdick for Herman Miller, Inc. Photo courtesy of Herman Miller, Inc. **156, 162–163**: Home offices from Techline. Photos courtesy of Techline: designed and manufactured by Marshall Erdman & Assoc. **157**, *top*: Seiko Berlitz Spanish/English Translator. **157**, *bottom*: Seiko Electronic Spell Checker. Photos courtesy of Seiko Instruments USA Inc. **158, 159**: Design by Bradley Rytz. Photo by Sharon Risedorph, courtesy of Bradley Rytz. **160**: Scooter® designed by Jack Kelley for Herman Miller, Inc. Photo by Bill Sharpe, courtesy of Herman Miller, Inc.**161**: Royal DM118 Electronic Organizer. Photo by NUVisions Studio, courtesy of Olivetti Office USA. **163**, bottom right: Geneva Tack Light from North Coast Medical, Inc. Photo

courtesy of North Coast Medical, Inc. **164**: HelloSet Cordless telephone. **165**: Vomax voice and fax mail system. Both available from Hello Direct Catalog of Telephone Productivity Tools. Photos courtesy of Hello Direct Catalog of Telephone Productivity Tools. **167**: Rubbermaid Seat Desk. Photo courtesy of Rubbermaid Office Products Inc. **168**: *Top left*: TD Collection designed by Tom Newhouse and Don Shepherd for Herman Miller, Inc. Photo by Elliott Kaufman, courtesy of Herman Miller, Inc. *Top right*: Turnstone home office furniture. Photo by Craig vanderLende, courtesy of Turnstone. Bottom left: Home Office Group from Sligh Furniture Co. Photo courtesy of Sligh Furniture Co.**168**, *bottom right*: Home office from Techline. Photo courtesy of Techline: designed and manufactured by Marshall Erdman & Assoc. **170, 171**: TD Collection designed by Tom Newhouse and Don Shepherd for Herman Miller, Inc. Photo by Elliott Kaufman, courtesy of Herman Miller,Inc. **172**: Relay® furniture designed by Geoff Hollington for Herman Miller, Inc. Photo by Phil Schaafsma, courtesy of Herman Miller, Inc. **173**: TD Collection designed by Tom Newhouse and Don Shepherd for Herman Miller, Inc. Photo by Nick Merrick, Hedrich-Blessing, courtesy of Herman Miller, Inc. **174**: *Top and bottom right*: Scooter® designed by Jack Kelley for Herman Miller, Inc. Photo by Earl Woods, courtesy of Herman Miller, Inc. Bottom left: Proper Chair, designed by Dragomir Ivicevic for Herman Miller, Inc. Photo courtesy of Herman Miller, Inc. **175**: Burdick Group designed by Bruce Burdick for Herman Miller, Inc. Photo courtesy of Herman Miller, Inc. **176**: Turnstone home office furniture. Photo by Craig vanderLende, courtesy of Turnstone. **177**: TS 315 chair from Turnstone. Photo by Craig vanderLende, courtesy of Turnstone. **178–181**: Techline home office components. Photos and drawing courtesy of Techline: designed and manufactured by Marshall Erdman & Assoc. **182,185**: Home Office Group from Sligh Furniture Co. Photo courtesy of Sligh Furniture Co. **183**: Drawing courtesy of Sligh Furniture Co. **184**: Computer Cabinet from Sligh Furniture Co. Photos courtesy of Sligh Furniture Co. **186–187**: Home/Suite/Office···2000®. Design by Joan Eisen, ASID. Photos courtesy of Joan Eisen, ASID. **188**: Avian™ office chair from Phoenix Designs, a subsidiary of Herman Miller, Inc. Photo courtesy of Herman Miller, Inc. **190**: Photos courtesy of Levenger "Tools for Serious Readers" Catalog Company. **191**, *top to bottom*: Photos courtesy of North Coast Medical, Inc.; Herman Miller, Inc.; and Turnstone (photos by Craig vanderLende). **192**, *top to bottom*: Photos courtesy of Apple

Computer, Inc. (photo by John Greenleigh); Herman Miller, Inc. (photo by Bill Sharpe); and Turnstone (photos by Craig vanderLende). **193**, *top to bottom*: Photos courtesy of Apple Computer, Inc. (photos by John Greenleigh); and Practical Peripherals. **194**: Photos courtesy of Canon USA, Inc. **195**, *top to bottom*: Photos courtesy of Mita Copystar America, Inc.; Sharp Electronics Corporation; and Xerox Corporation. **196**: TD Collection designed by Tom Newhouse and Don Shepherd for Herman Miller, Inc. Photos by Elliott Kaufman, courtesy of Herman Miller, Inc. **197**, *top to bottom*: Photos courtesy of Levenger "Tools for Serious Readers" Catalog Company; Rubbermaid Office Products Inc.; and Turnstone (photo by Craig vanderLende). **198**: Photos courtesy of North Coast Medical, Inc. **199**, *top to bottom*: Photos courtesy of North Coast Medical, Inc.; and Turnstone (photo by Craig vanderLende). **200**, *top to bottom*: Photos courtesy of Canon USA, Inc.; Samsung Electronics America, Inc.; Sanyo Office Automation; and Sharp Electronics Corporation. **201**, *top*: Reprint permission granted by AOL. All rights reserved. **201**, bottom: Photo courtesy of Hello Direct Catalog of Telephone Productivity Tools. **202**: Photos courtesy of Hello Direct Catalog of Telephone Productivity Tools. **203**: Photos courtesy of Levenger "Tools for Serious Readers" Catalog Company. **204**, *top to bottom*: Photos courtesy of Paper Access; and Paper Direct, Inc. **205**, *top to bottom*: Photos courtesy of Paper Direct, Inc.; and Sanyo Office Automation. **206**: *Top*: Photo provided by AT&T Consumer Products. Bottom: Photo courtesy of Hello Direct Catalog of Telephone Productivity Tools. **207**, *top to bottom*: Photos courtesy of Hello Direct Catalog of Telephone Productivity Tools; Motorola Cellular Subscriber Group; and Sharp Electronics Corporation. Memo Express™ is a trademark of Motorola, Inc. **208**, *top to bottom*: Photos courtesy of Canon USA, Inc.; Olivetti Office USA; and Sanyo Office Automation. **209**, *top to bottom*: Photos courtesy of Seiko Instruments USA Inc.; and Sharp Electronics Corporation. **210**, *top to bottom*: Photos courtesy of Apple Computer, Inc. (photo by John Greenleigh) ; and Epson America, Inc. **211**, *top to bottom*: Photos courtesy of Hewlett-Packard; and Seiko Instruments USA Inc. **212**, top: Reprinted with permission from Entrepreneur Magazine. **212**, *bottom*: Reprinted by permission from Home Office Computing. **213**: Photo courtesy of Office Depot. **214**: Photos courtesy of Canon USA, Inc. **215**, *top to bottom*: Photos courtesy of Davis Furniture Industries, Inc.; and Ergotron. **216**: Photo courtesy of Hello Direct Catalog of Telephone Productivity Tools.

INDEX